Manor
Minor Press

Moving Freely Forward

Manor
Minor Press

Moving Freely Forward
A Handbook for Training Level Dressage

Krister Swartz

Illustrations by Miranda Ottewell

List of Illustrations

Contents

Acknowledgments

Not only did my wife, Miranda Ottewell, support my writing of this little handbook, spend countless evenings discussing riding theory, and take on extra farm chores while I sat at my keyboard, she also honed her drawing skills and produced all of the illustrations for this project, as well as copy-editing the text. It can only be an understatement to say that without her this project would never have been completed. And to have been able to complete it with someone whom I love was an unearned bonus.

I would like to ask everyone who reads this book to take a moment to recognize the thousands of people around the country who volunteer their time, energy, and skills to steer our GMOs, organize and manage countless schooling and recognized shows, and then show up to make those shows happen. Without scribes, stewards, runners, scorers, people who set up arenas and then take them down again, announcers, maintenance people, sound engineers, and those in the offices who check riders in, handle emergencies, tabulate and post final score sheets, among many other volunteers, we quite literally would not have this sport in America. The next time you are at a show, take a moment to thank a volunteer.

The USDF works tirelessly to promote our sport. Through their support, a number of clinics, symposia, scholarships, and other educational avenues are made possible. I would in particular like to draw attention to the world-class "L" judge-training program, and to thank all of the faculty and judges from whom I had the honor to learn while going through this program.

I have learned a great deal from all the horses that I have had a chance to work with. But I am often reminded of one or another of a number of low-level school horses I met when first learning to ride. What they taught me about riding basics and their patience with my ineptitude has stayed with me through the years. It is to my shame that I cannot list them all here by name.

Introduction

In 1949, a lone horse-and-rider pair entered the pitch-dark stadium of White City, in London, surrounded and followed by four bright spotlights. The rider was a gifted horseman from the recently fallen Austro-Hungarian Empire; the horse was a Lipizzaner by the name of Neapolitano Africa. In front of a packed crowd they rode their program in a bubble of light that extended just two feet around them. Only when the arena perimeter appeared in this light did they know that they had run out of room; flowerpots along the perimeter were the only clue as to where they might be. At all other times, they were essentially riding blind.

That a horse and rider can perform the upper-level movements of piaffe, passage, and canter pirouettes at all is of course remarkable. But how much more incredible to command in a horse such straightness, such mathematical precision in the lateral work, and such correct and unswaying lead changes so as never to miss a flowerpot marker and go entirely off course! Add to this the trust and confidence a horse and rider must have in each other, to set out at an extended trot or canter into utter darkness. A storm of applause greeted the pair when they came to a halt.

Alois Podhajsky relates this experience in his wonderful book *My Horses, My Teachers.* Shortly after this ride at White City, Podhajsky came down with a severe bout of hepatitis, and later that year Neapolitano Africa caught a mortal lung disease. Though Podhajsky would recover, to spend many years as director of the Spanish Riding School in Vienna, that night in London was the pinnacle of success for that horse-and-rider pair.

I think of this story almost every day. I try to allow my mind to concentrate on and my body to feel all the subtle changes in movement and balance in myself and in the horse beneath me as if I too were riding in utter darkness. I try to use my mind's eye to see patterns, even the entire pattern of a dressage test, and myself and my horse within those patterns, following and creating the flow at the same time. And I wonder not at the advanced movements of upper-level horses, but at just how amazing it is to ride a simple straight line or a perfect twenty-meter circle.

This volume hopes to encourage a deep appreciation for riding that straight line and perfect circle. These are the basics, the fundamentals, of dressage riding. The straight line and the circle are found at all levels of dressage riding and competition. It is important to make the point again: the circle and the straight line are fundamental to all dressage riding. And to ride them well and correctly takes discipline, feeling, and practice. Podhajsky will always be a greater rider than any of us, but we can all feel a part of that greatness—not by riding the piaffe, but by honing our fundamentals to a point where after riding an exemplary twenty-meter circle, we can say to ourselves: Maybe, just maybe, I could have done that in the dark.

I also hope that this handbook can help any horse-and-rider pair to compete successfully in the training level tests through the use of proper horsemanship. It is not a collection of tricks and short cuts to the sole end of acquiring blue ribbons, but a tutoring guide built on a belief that the dressage tests as laid out by the U.S. Equestrian Federation have been created in a way that supports and rewards correct and beautiful riding. When we follow the training steps inherent in these tests, we also follow in the footsteps of great horse-and-rider pairs like Colonel Alois Podhajsky and Neapolitano Africa.

Part 1 of this volume discusses a number of general principles that should be foremost in the rider's mind at this level. There are many great books on dressage riding, most if not all of them taking in the great breadth of riding from intro to grand prix. In the end, each book spends very little time on any one level of riding. Reading about upper-level movements can be inspiring, but this volume confines itself to training level only, to give this very important foundation for the higher levels the focus it deserves.

Part 2, "From the Judge's Box," explains in some depth what the judge is looking for in a training level horse and rider, and the methodology used to arrive at your score.

In part 3, I offer a number of gymnastic exercises for horse and rider, which can be used both to advance training generally and as a preparation for the training level tests. Obviously, these are just a few of many valuable exercises; I include them here to encourage you to think about how each ride fits with your overall pathway through the level.

The brief lunging primer that comprises part 4 is fundamentally concerned with understanding what we see when we watch a horse at work, and can therefore be of interest even to those who do not lunge.

In part 5, I first dissect the individual movements that are combined in various ways to make up the three 2011 USDF training level tests. I then go through each test movement by movement, giving tips on how to segue from one to the next. You can use this as an aid while you visualize riding the test, or even have someone read it aloud to you as you practice your test. It's not the same as having your own trainer there, but few of us have that luxury every ride, and it will give you something to focus on other than your horse's ears.

Part 1

General Principles

While it is exciting to read about and dream of the movements and theory of the upper levels, it is impossible to overstress the importance of the foundation represented by the training level tests. Take this foundation seriously, and try not to get ahead of yourself in your riding. Focus on preparing yourself physically, like any athlete, and laying down the groundwork for yourself and your horse. To ask for a leg yield, you must first have an independent seat; to understand and feel impulsion in the horse, you must first understand and feel a relaxed rhythm. Be humble and clear about your abilities as a rider, and appreciate the discipline, patience, hard work, and skill involved in riding at training level. Remember: the horse cannot lie. If you do not master these basics now, you will certainly have to return to them; just when you think you are ready to advance from third level to fourth level, for example, you will instead end up relinquishing your double bridle and entering at A at a working trot.

The Purpose of the Training Level Tests

The USDF dressage tests are designed in accordance with the basic

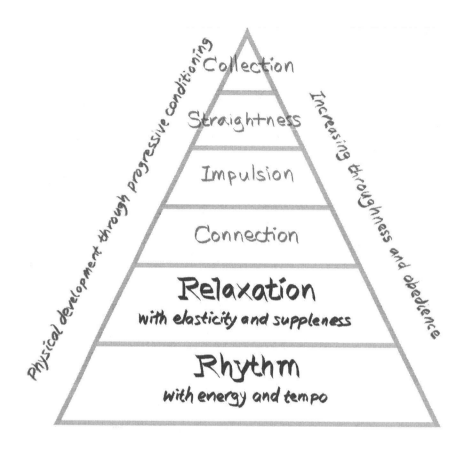

Figure 1. The Training Scale

principles of the training scale, commonly presented as the pyramid of training, or the training pyramid (fig. 1).

An example of the depths of wisdom found in this simple diagram, which reflects centuries of refinement by a long line of past masters, is immediately apparent when we look at the first, bottom step of the pyramid. Notice that rhythm, not relaxation, is called for first. Isn't that odd? It seems that we should have our horse relaxed before asking anything more of him. But the training pyramid clearly puts rhythm first.

To understand why, ask yourself: How do we get a horse to relax? How do we ask him to be calm and focused? First, we must start with the simplest request; we must clear all the clutter away and give him something easy to understand. For example, ask him simply to trot in a twenty-meter circle. He need not think of anything else but continuing in this circle. Our job as rider and trainer is to see to it that he travels this circle and does not go wide at one point and cut in at another. All attempts on his part to complicate matters must be headed off. He must also learn to travel on this circle at a consistent tempo, not rushing at one point and slowing down at another. Again, we mustn't let him complicate the situation. And here we arrive at the base of the training pyramid, rhythm.

We must first create a space, a safe zone, for the horse. We must patiently show him that he need not fear, nor question, nor anticipate anything more complicated than a simple trot in a clear rhythm at an even tempo. Once he has understood this, the horse can relax; he knows now that nothing more will be asked. So it is rhythm that creates relaxation in the horse.

Let us take a closer look at the terms rhythm, relaxation, and connection, as these concepts will be your focus at training level. At the 2005 USDF convention, the faculties of the USDF's "L" judge training and instructor certification programs met to clarify the English translations of the original German words used in the training pyramid. After a year of work, J. Ashton Moore printed the fruit of their labors in an article in the *USDF Connection,* the official publication of the U.S. Dressage Federation, and that article informs much of what will be presented here.

To better understand the word *rhythm* as applied to the training pyramid, we must recognize that its German equivalent, *Takt*, embraces in its meaning not only the regularity or purity of the gaits but also their tempo. It is not enough that a horse lug itself around the arena at a snail's pace, even if its rhythm is regular. A horse with rhythm is moving forward energetically, in a pure and regular gait. To understand how he should be using himself as he moves brings us to the second stage of the pyramid: relaxation.

With the introduction of relaxation (from the German *Losgelassenheit*) into the mix we begin to address the horse's mind as well as his body. When applied to his body a distinction must be made between "relaxed" and "limp" or "floppy"; relaxation implies positive muscle tone, through which the horse becomes elastic and supple. It implies a state free of negative muscle tone, or "blocks," in the horse. Think of a well-designed sliding door or kitchen drawer that slides smoothly back and forth, as opposed to one that grabs and screeches.

When applied to his mind, relaxation in a horse should be understood in terms more of focus than calmness. The mind of a relaxed horse is attentive and willing, not dull and vacant, so that he becomes an active partner. In his *Grundzuge der Reitkunst* (1951; reprint, New York: Olms, 1996) lieutenant colonel Gustav von Dreyhausen gives an insightful explanation: "We can therefore perhaps characterize correct equestrian *Losgelassenheit* as a type of behavior in which the horse yields completely to the rider's aids and applies all of his strength and all of his muscles towards the energetic and impulsive execution of the present demands without feeling constricted."

Anlehnung is the German word for the third step of the training pyramid. The translation of this word as "contact" in English renditions of the training pyramid has caused great damage to dressage riding in America, for two reasons. First, it puts the focus on bit contact and with it the position of the horse's head; second, it gives no hint of the lively and rewarding interplay between horse and rider when the rider establishes a real connection between the hind end and the front of the horse and between her own hips and hands. The new translation, "Connection (acceptance of the bit through acceptance of the aids)," is likely to do more to improve matters than any number of clinics across the nation. I will discuss this concept at length in "Bit Contact," below.

Keeping these three basic levels of the training pyramid in mind, we can then return to the training level tests. As the U.S. Equestrian Federation states on the test itself, the purpose of the training level tests is "to confirm that the horse's muscles are supple and loose and that it moves freely forward in a clear and steady rhythm." The rider's goal for training level, then, is to supple the horse and guide him accurately through the gymnastic patterns of the tests in a consistent rhythm, allowing and encouraging him to move forward. Don't get too wrapped up in whether the horse is "in a frame." Concentrate on building the firm foundation of riding a horse that is mentally calm and willing, and physically supple.

How is this correct riding mirrored in the tests? If you look over the three training level tests, you will notice that of all the movements, only the free walk and the "stretchy circle" are marked as a coefficient—that is, the score earned for them is doubled—wherever they appear. Out of the total ten coefficients in all the training tests combined, six of them are given for these two movements, which are precisely the ones that best highlight relaxation and rhythm.

The remaining four coefficients are given to canter movements. A green horse new to dressage competition will most likely show its tension—that is, its loss of relaxation and thus rhythm—when it is asked to canter. But it is interesting that the canter coefficients don't turn up until the second test. The first test asks for the canter circles, but not until the second test is the score for them doubled; here we see how the tests are designed to keep some of the pressure off the horse-and-rider pair. Similarly, while test 2 gives coefficients for the canter circles themselves, test 3 places them on the more exacting transitions into canter.

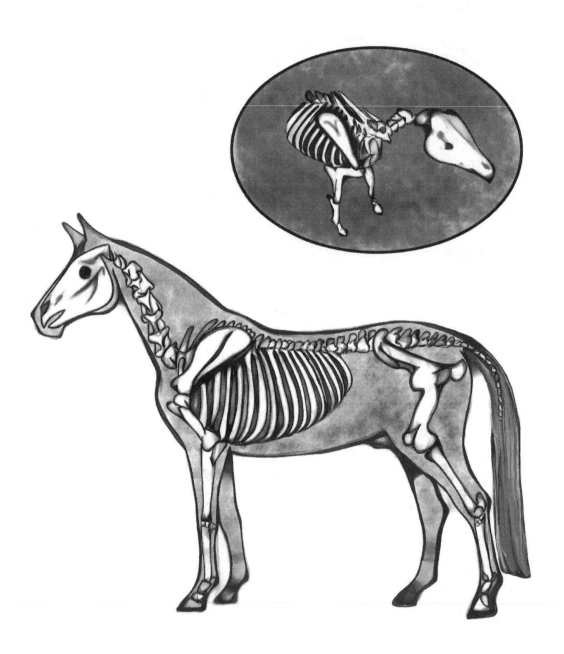

Figure 2. The Skeleton of the Horse, with Detail of the Scapula

The Circle of Muscles

An understanding of the horse's skeletal and muscular structure is fundamental to properly influencing his balance and movement.

From the perspective of riding, the most important and interesting thing about the horse's skeleton is that his forelegs and shoulder blades are not attached to the rest of his skeleton (fig. 2). Horses do not have collarbones that attach their forelegs and shoulder blades to their neck and rib cage; instead, only a group of muscles connects the horse's scapula to its ribs. Along with the neck muscles, these muscles not only allow the horse's front legs to move forward and backward and to some extent sideways but also allow him to raise his withers and the base of his neck relative to his front legs, shifting his balance. This is an extremely important aspect of the horse's anatomy, and we will return to it.

The muscular system that moves the horse's bones is commonly referred to as the "ring of muscles" or "circle of muscles," first described by master horseman Gustav Steinbrecht in his Gymnasium of the Horse, published in Germany in 1886. When these muscles work properly together, no single muscle or muscle group is over- or underused. Incorrect riding, however, disrupts the coherent harmony of these muscles and not only stimulates incorrect muscle development but can often lead to injury. This can be seen easily enough in a horse that travels with its neck bulging on the underside, hollow areas directly behind and in front of the top of the shoulder blades, and a generally bony appearance along an undeveloped topline.

To better understand proper movement, let's follow one complete rotation of the circle (fig. 3). The hindquarters are the horse's engine; here all thrusting power originates. The muscles that run down the front of the thigh bone bring each hind leg forward and set it on the ground, but they are not used to push the horse forward. This is done with the muscles of the croup, the hip, and the back of the hindquarters. The upper muscles of the hip and croup are connected to the long muscles of the back and the deep muscles of the spine, which are in turn connected to the muscles of the flank and upper neck. This chain from the hind legs and haunches up over the horse's back and from there to the poll is the top half of the ring of muscles. The movement of the horse literally comes from the rippling effect of the flexing and relaxing of these muscles over the horse's back. Anything that interferes with this movement will cause poor movement in the horse. This is why the saddle must fit the horse's back properly, without pinching or sitting too hard on his withers and spine. An unbalanced or rigid rider will also impede this movement over the back, as will hands that pull back on the reins and cause the neck to stiffen. These interferences will cause the horse to hollow his back, which in turn will keep his hind legs out behind him, where they cannot push off well.

Now we come back to the muscles of the horse's shoulder. These muscles, known as the "thoracic sling," are capable of raising the withers and the base of the neck slightly; then, in turn, the front legs can move more freely. This mechanism facilitates both extension, by allowing the legs a greater range of movement, and collection, by helping to shift the horse's balance back to his hind end.

The thoracic sling begins the second half of the circle of muscles, which is completed by the abdominal muscles. These muscles run from the breastbone to the bottom of the pelvis. They support the horse's gut, help him to breathe, and enable him to flex his pelvis, bringing his hindquarters under him. They are helped by the psoas muscles, which run from the underside of the spine to the pelvis and to each thigh bone. These muscles, by contracting the belly and flexing the pelvis, and thereby dropping the croup, allow the hind legs to reach farther underneath the horse, setting the horse back on his haunches and giving the hind legs more purchase for a stronger strike-off.

To recap: The hind leg reaches deep under the horse, because his croup

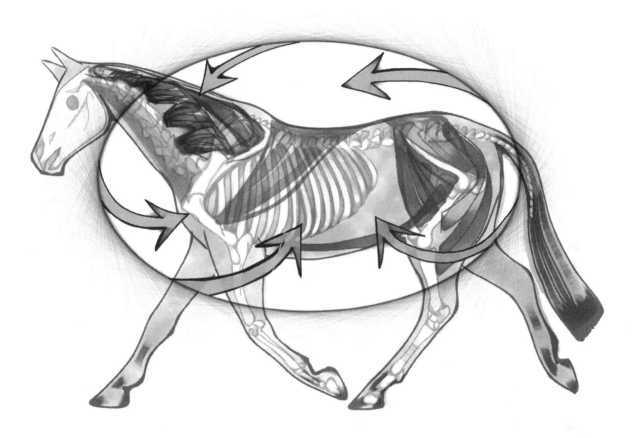

Figure 3. The Circle of Muscles

has dropped, allowing him to push off with great strength. The movement passes over the horse's back, which is raised and strong due to the pull along the spine from poll to croup, much like a suspension bridge. The shoulder and neck muscles raise the withers, and the abdominal muscles contract, lifting the horse's back and dropping his croup, so that his hind legs can reach deep underneath.

Moderating and Directing the Flow

Have in your mind a side view of a training level horse in motion at the walk. Mark how his body moves, not just his legs but his haunches, back, withers, neck, and stomach, with particular attention to the motion through his back. Now, as he is walking, mentally place a rider on him, and envision how this rider's body must move through her legs, hips, stomach, back, and neck in order to flow with the horse's movement. While you are watching these two move together in your mind, switch the angle to a view from behind the horse and rider and observe how both the horse and rider move together. Go back to the side view, and when the horse takes the trot, watch how his body's movement changes with the gait. How does the rider's body change to match him? When you switch again to the view from behind, what do you see? And when he then takes the canter, and a different set of movements, use both your side view and view from behind to determine how the rider's body again changes to match him.

This idealized rider flows with her horse, and once the connection has been established between the two bodies, she begins to accentuate the flow in her body to direct the horse's movement and balance. First she learns to flow with the horse in each gait, then she develops the ability to redirect the flow in her body to create transitions between and within the gaits in the horse rather than through tensions and blocking in her body that impedes the horse's energy and freedom. And finally, through this ability she begins to effect a change in the horse's balance as he progresses in his training up through the levels.

The act of riding is the governance of the horse's energy, the horse's balance, the rider's energy, and the rider's balance. Only when the rider understands how to ride the horse through her ability to receive, develop, influence, and direct the horse's energy flow without negative tension and locked joints in her own body, which in turn create locks and blockages in the horse, will she attain throughness in herself and her horse. When we then talk of the rider's position, her use of her core muscles, and the mechanics of her seat in motion, whether sitting at any gait or posting to the trot, we are trying to understand how to best position our body to allow us to take part in and direct this flow through the horse. Our goal in striving for the correct position, posture, and balance on the horse is not to create negative tension in our bodies but to create an elasticity and suppleness in our bodies that we may then impart to our horses.

The Rider's Position

For the training level horse to move properly, before we can ask any more from him, he must first deal with the added weight of the rider on his back, a task made even harder when this added weight is itself out of balance. A vital part of achieving relaxation and rhythm in a horse is making it easier for him, physically and mentally, to deal with this new weight.

Ideally, the horse should be prepared in advance for this task, which is why work in hand and lunging are so useful for the horse embarking on a dressage career, even if he has been ridden extensively in another discipline or as a trail horse. The dressage discipline requires a horse to use muscles in a new way, or use ones he may not have used before. But even if he is given the chance to prepare himself for the added weight of a rider, more importantly, the rider must also learn to sit properly on the horse's back.

The first step in helping a horse to cope with added weight is to learn how to sit on him properly. Just as the beginning dressage horse should be schooled with the first two steps of the training pyramid always in mind, a training level rider should also concentrate on relaxing and suppling her own body and mind. And just as lunging a horse is a beneficial way to start a dressage horse, lunging the rider is an excellent way to establish the proper fundamentals of seat position and balance. Since many of us do not have this luxury, we must be doubly diligent during our time in the saddle. Think less at this point about how you might one day piaffe, and more about learning to relax your body and engaging your core abdominal muscles. And remember that just as relaxation in the horse does not mean that he should go limp, relaxation for the rider also means the toning of the body and the elasticizing of the muscles to create a supple body in proper position and balance. In fact, much of your time on a horse at this point should be focused on your own position and balance, and how this position and balance can allow the horse to move freely forward. This is very important for both you and your horse; time spent on these basics now will repay you amply later.

Relaxing requires an active effort. The first time we sat on a horse and it began to walk, our instinct was to tense our bodies in a defensive manner. We closed our chest, hunched our shoulders, and clung on with our hands. As we "learned to ride" and became more accustomed to the horse, we lost our initial defensive state of mind. However, what most of us did not do was also release that initial defensive tension in our body. As time went by, we concentrated on how to make the horse do what we wanted it to do. Our first lessons centered on how to make the horse go, how to make him stop, how to turn him left and right, and so on. Through this process, we learned to cope with the tension in our body, and minimized its effects on our mind. And because we are rational creatures, this was enough to allow us to control our emotions and gain confidence in our ability to impose our will on the horse.

Just as relaxation in the horse concerns releasing the tension in the "wrong" muscles and developing strength and tone in the "correct" ones, we as riders must understand relaxation to be releasing the old defensive tension and other tensions that extend from it, which paradoxically hinder correct riding, and developing our core muscles, the ones that make us stronger, more secure riders. The trick to doing this is to stop merely imposing our will on the horse, and instead develop our ability to feel the

Figure 4. The Rider as Beacon

horse's body under us.

To attain this relaxation, you will need to reverse the way your body has been working. You will need to search out all of the muscles in your body and begin relaxing them. At the same time you will need to concentrate on your core muscles, the muscles you need to tone or flex to stay balanced on the horse. But remember that unconsciously you will begin to tighten all those unnecessary muscles again, so that you must constantly remind yourself to relax them. Think of your body as a mansion with lights on in every room. Only the room you are in needs to be lit, so you must go through the mansion, turn off all the lights, and return to that one lit room. But the mansion is also haunted by ghosts that love to turn lights on, so you'll have to make several more trips around the place, turning off lights yet again. Sooner or later the poltergeists will tire of this game, but until then you will have to be diligent.

While you are turning out all the unnecessary lights, you will also be developing your core muscles into a beacon that illuminates the way forward (Fig. 4).

In the illustration that follows of a rider in correct alignment (fig. 5), notice how the "building blocks" of the rider's body—legs, pelvis, torso, head—are stacked one on top of the other in perfect balance. A straight line can be drawn from the shoulders through the hips and down to the heel. The rider's arms rest at her sides, her hands are held in front of her belly button, and her eyes are up and looking out and forward. From a back view, her shoulders are horizontally even; she does not collapse to one side or the other at the waist; her legs rest evenly on each side of the horse's flank, and her toes point forward, not out. Remember that this is an ideal, and that you are unlikely to have achieved this ideal yet. It will take time and constant attention to achieve and maintain a balanced position, but the effort now will pay manyfold in the future as you move up the levels. Remember also that this is a static image of the correct position. The correct position is one that allows the pelvis to rock slightly so that the movement of the horse's back can more easily travel up through the rider's spine. When you ride, your body will be constantly adjusting as it deals with the movement of the horse.

Using Your Core

The very heart of correct position is the strength of the inner core mus-

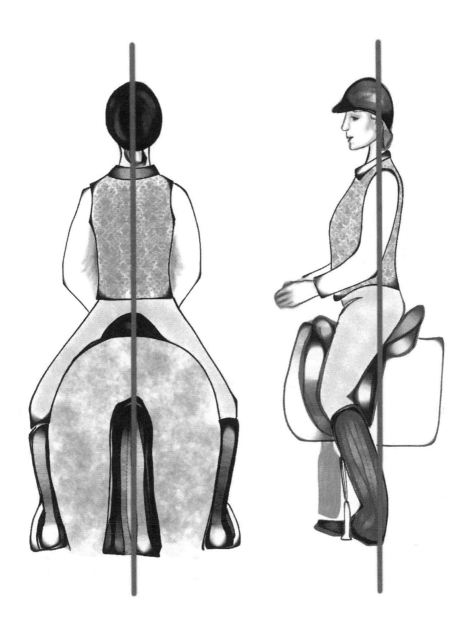

Figure 5. Rider in Alignment, from the Back and Side

cles, your abdominals. These are the muscles that you must engage, when lunged without reins or stirrups, to sit properly balanced on the horse without using your shoulders, arms, or legs for added support.

To begin developing your core muscles, try coughing or growling, and concentrate on what muscles are working in your body. Notice that doing this creates a downward and outward push in your abdomen, as if you are sending your weight downward. This helps us "plug in" to the horse's back.

Riding from your core will also free your arms and legs to act independently, and consequently allow you to give clear aids to the horse. If you use your arms and reins to help you lift off the saddle while posting to the trot, it is impossible for your horse to develop a good relationship with the bit. If you hold on to the horse with the reins, it will be very difficult to combine your leg and rein aids to ask for a leg yield. If your right leg is tight against the horse and your left leg hangs away from his side, imagine the trouble you will have asking him to canter in a circle to the right without your left leg there to support his haunches, or to the left without your left leg to maintain forward movement.

While strengthening your core muscles, pay close attention to the position of your pelvis, which must be aligned correctly to play its proper role in the tower of building blocks. Look at the four diagrams of the pelvis and thigh in figure 6. The first (a) shows the top of the pelvis tilted forward in the "fork seat," a position that hollows the rider's back and can tip her torso forward out of balance. In the second diagram (b), the pelvis is tilted backward in the "armchair" position, which creates a soft, slumped back and tends to put the legs too far forward to support the rider in balance.

The third diagram (c) depicts a pelvis in the balanced, neutral position. Although this neutral position is important, by itself it is not enough. In the last diagram (d), the rider's pelvis is again aligned correctly; but here, in addition, her thighs are stretched down. Here we come to an important aspect of the effective seat: the angle made by the pelvis and thigh bones,

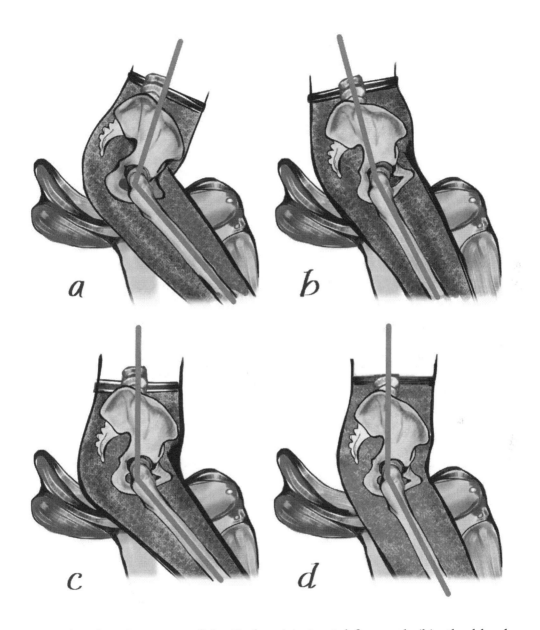

Figure 6. Pelvic Position of the Rider: (a) tipped forward; (b) tilted back;
(c) neutral; (d) neutral with thigh stretched down

Figure 7. The Rider as Bow and Arrow

which tends to be too closed in the fork seat, and too open in the armchair seat. When this angle can be opened while the pelvis remains neutral, however, the rider will be able to maintain her torso above her pelvis, with her pelvis aligned in the neutral position, and at the same time keep her legs down and back underneath her. To do this the rider must relax her adductor muscles, those muscles on the inside of the thigh that when used incorrectly grip the horse. Using these muscles (often referred to as "pinching") will pop us out of the saddle, as well as blocking the movement of the horse's back.

Think of this angle when you are riding. If your instructor asks you to put your shoulders back, she will probably soon after remind you to put your legs underneath you. And soon after that, she will again tell you to put your shoulders back, and so on. This teeter-tottering will continue forever if you do not think instead of opening this pelvic angle and leading with your belly button. One tip could be to think of yourself as a bow that is drawn back to fire an arrow. Both the top and bottom ends stretch back as the middle section is pushed forward (fig. 7).

Though we often hear talk of making our legs long and stretching them down, don't think that you can drop your stirrups five holes in a day. Long stirrups are something that must be earned, by opening the angle made by your pelvis and thigh. And this will only occur as you work to stretch the tendons that tend to close that angle, and allow the legs to lengthen as a result. Pushing our legs down often causes us to push our feet forward and lock this hip/thigh angle even more.

Feel the stretch in the front of your thigh, as if you were starting to kneel. A command all too often heard in the arena is "Heels down." Think instead of pushing your knees down and back. Again, if you think of pushing your heels down, you will almost always end up by pushing your legs forward and closing your pelvic angle. You will also make the ankle joint stiff, instead of supple and flexible, as it should be. If instead

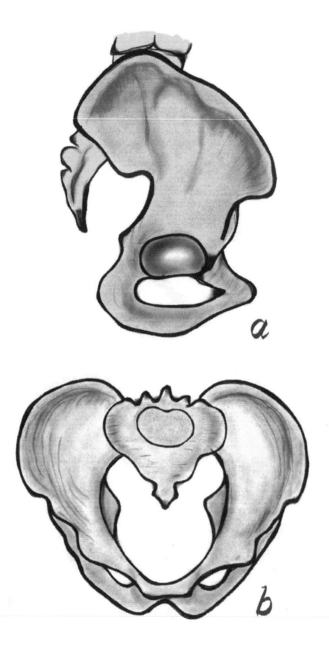

Figure 8. View of pelvis from the side (a) and from above (b)

you open the pelvic angle, stretch the front of your thighs, and push your knees down, you will keep your leg in its proper place under you, while at the same time keeping it supple.

The Seat in Motion

It is all well and good to talk about the perfect seat on a horse and to examine static drawings of correct position, but in real life the horse is moving, and so are you. Thus, we must apply what we know about alignment and balance to the horse and rider in motion.

We use a number of expressions when talking about how a rider's body should influence the horse's balance and movement. Unfortunately, few of them explain or describe in detail what it is we are supposed to do.

And when a writer does attempt a proper explanation, it is often off the mark. Take for example Wilhelm Müseler's fantastic book of 1933 (translated into English in 1937 as *Riding Logic*). In it, Müseler goes to some pain to underscore the importance of this ability to follow the horse's back, and gives a number of wonderful visual examples of how to use your body. However, he explains the action as that of using the back muscles, and his expression "das Kreuz anzehen" is translated as "bracing the back." But it is not our back muscles we are using; it is our core.

Let's look again at a diagram of the pelvis (fig. 8). Note that, from a side view (a), the underside of our pelvic bones (made up of the ischial ramus, the pubic ramus, and the ischial tuberosity) is somewhat curved. A top view (b) also shows that the bones we sit on are not parallel, but come closer toward the front. To maintain a straight line from our ears, through our hips, and down to our ankle, we must learn to rock ever so slightly back and forth along this curve when riding the walk, the canter, and the sitting trot.

Think of how your pelvis moves and your core muscles work as you push a swing. Or, as Müseler suggests, if you stand in front of a table with a book resting on the table but projecting from it, you can push the book wholly onto the table with your hips. He also points out that if you sit on a narrow, light stool, with legs apart, as if on a horse, you can tilt the stool forward.

Unfortunately, of course, he says we do this by bracing the back. What we do, actually, is engage our core muscles to tilt the pelvis. We do not use our back muscles. When we engage these core muscles to rock the pelvis, our back will flatten and curve in again—hence Müseler's expression. But the back is flattening because the pelvis is tilting, due to the use of our core muscles, not to any use of our back muscles. Or rather, our back muscles stretch because of our use of our core muscles.

It is imperative that we understand that the muscles we must use are those deep in the abdomen, and that the movement will be like pulling your lower intestines back to your spine. When we are thus balanced on a pelvis that is allowed to rock slightly with the horse's motion, we are "plugged in" to the horse's back. We become one with the motion of the horse's back, and thus in a position to truly influence it.

But there is still one more element. We must also have the coordination to move our hips separately, to follow the movement of the horse's hips. We must allow our hips to swing with the horse's movement, and when one side of the horse needs to be encouraged, we must be able to swing one hip more than the other.

Think of sitting on the horse at the walk. As the horse places his weight on the inside hind leg, we will feel an upward bulging motion under our inside seat bone, which we must not block with a rigid pelvis. When the horse then lifts his inside hind leg off the ground, we will feel that side sinking, and must have the flexibility to allow our pelvis to sink with this. This means that one side of our seat, let us say the inside, will be making room for the lifting of the horse's hip while the other side, the outside, will be reaching down to follow the dip of the other hip, and then the inside seat will have to reach down while the outside makes room, and so on.

In the canter the rider's seat and hips must also follow the motion of the horse's hips. However, since here the horse's inside hind leg must come up and take the weight in the canter stride, the rider's inside seat bone, or hip, must move slightly forward if it is not to block this movement. The outside hip will move back slightly, naturally. The movement in the rider's seat at the canter is akin to how we use our hips while skipping.

I will take up the mechanics of sitting to the trot in the companion volume to this one, which covers first level. In this volume we will concentrate on the mechanics of the rising trot.

The Rising Trot

In the rising trot, the pelvis is lifted off the horse as it is pushed forward and then comes back down to rest on the saddle. Let's take a closer look at just what is happening at the rising trot with the rider, and how she can work to make her post more effective.

When the horse sets out at the trot, the ripple over his back caused by his haunches pushing off throws the rider somewhat forward in the saddle. This is the cue for the rider to lift out of the saddle, using the horse's own movement to help her in the first upward part of the rising trot. But there are two ripples over the horse's back, one caused by the inside hind leg pushing off and the other by the outside hind leg.

The beginning rider is commonly taught to lift off the saddle as the horse's outside front leg is coming forward. This is because many beginners cannot feel what is happening with the horse's back legs at any given time, but can easily look down at the horse's shoulders. At the trot, the horse moves his diagonal pairs at the same time. That is, when his inside hind leg is moving forward, his outside front leg is too. So when he brings his outside front leg forward, his inside hind leg also comes forward. Since the inside hind leg bears more weight in a turn or on a circle, it is kinder for the rider to follow this movement, so that her weight comes down on the horse as his load-bearing leg is on the ground and better able to support this extra weight. Rising on this diagonal (outside fore, inside hind) makes it easier for the horse to balance himself correctly.

Understanding these biomechanics also helps us to understand why a horse may regularly "throw" you onto one posting diagonal or another, regardless of what direction you are traveling, or why it might feel easier to post on one diagonal than another. There you are, going along, and suddenly you realize that you are on the wrong diagonal, or you change rein, and suddenly your posting doesn't seem as easy or smooth. Since every horse is stronger on one side and weaker on the other, the push off from behind will be slightly different for each hind leg. This unevenness in the horse will diminish as correct riding strengthens both sides evenly and equally. One way to test your horse for crookedness is to switch diagonals while riding along the long side, and feel the difference. This is also a good exercise to practice when out on a long, straight trail. Remember, however, to take into account that every rider is also "one-sided," and you may prefer one diagonal regardless of your horse's evenness or lack thereof.

While taking the cue for rising out of the saddle from the horse's movement, also be attentive to the horse's natural thrust. If you do not match this thrust sufficiently, you will end up being a drag on the horse. And if you attempt to post at a faster rate than the horse's natural rhythm, you will end up compromising this rhythm.

To understand how to rise, we must return to the base position discussed earlier. When the rider is balanced properly over the horse, a vertical line can be drawn from the shoulders, through the hip, and down to the ankle bone and heel. This "plumb line" shifts slightly forward in the rising trot, so that the ball of the foot becomes the bottom point, rather than the ankle or heel. This is because the rider will need to shift her hips forward slightly in the rising part of the trot.

When the rider has learned successfully to balance her upper body over this shifting support base, she will be able to use her hands and arms independently, instead of pulling on the horse's mouth to lift herself up off the saddle, and she will also be able to relax her legs so that they do not grip too tightly to the horse or dig too deeply into the stirrups.

To better understand this, sit in an upright chair with your knees bent at a ninety-degree angle and your feet flat on the floor. To rise out of the chair, you will need to bring your hands out in front of you or set them on your knees for support. If you were on a horse, this would translate into pulling yourself up with your reins, and thereby pulling on the horse's mouth. If you slide your feet back underneath the chair, and consequently under your center of gravity, however, you will not need your arms and upper body to rise from the chair. Now try to rise from the chair with your arms by your side and your feet back out in front of you; what you will probably experience is a hopping or jumping attempt that only lands you back down hard on your seat. If you were riding, you would slam down hard on the horse's back.

This little experiment highlights two very important aspects of a correct post. First, the rising trot is basically two general movements: the movement of the hips over the shifted support base of the ball of the foot, and the return of the hips and seat to the saddle, with a resulting shift of balance back over the ankle bone or heel. It is important that this second half be performed so that you smoothly and gently touch down the horse's back, and don't just relax and plop down on it.

Think of your thigh as a lever whose fulcrum is the knee. When you rise, this lever lifts your hips forward. And it is this lever that gently lowers you back to the saddle in the second half of the post sequence. While it is the thigh and lower torso muscles that perform this movement, it is important that your abdominal, stomach, and side muscles be kept firm, preventing you from lengthening the front of your body and hollowing

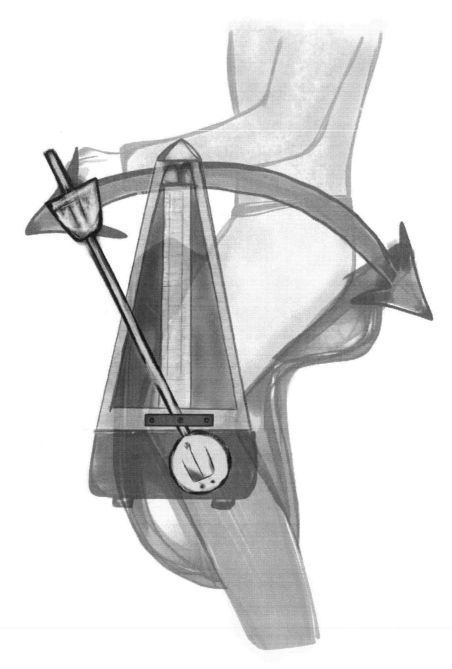

Figure 9. The Thigh as a Metronome in Rising Trot

your back as you rise. Your torso should act as one solid block that is levered up and down through the working of your pelvic joint and the opening of your pelvic angle. It should feel as if you are keeping your body balanced and still, as your pelvic region swings mostly forward and only slightly upward.

The chair exercise also reveals a second important aspect of the rising trot: when you attempted to rise out of the chair with your feet in front and your arms at your side, the lift that you were able to achieve came not from below, but from your chest, shoulder, and neck muscles. This would be akin to a horse traveling above the bit, his head stuck up in the air, the bottom of his neck bulging, and his back hollow. The correct post results from swinging your hips forward from the thigh, so that the pelvic angle widens as you rise and closes as you sit.

Do not think so much of coming up as you post, since this will cause you to heave yourself out of the saddle with your upper body muscles. Think instead of pushing your hips forward. The thigh bone lever with its fulcrum at the knee is angled slightly back toward the horse's hindquarters. Since the thigh bone stays a consistent length, when it swings forward, its upper end, connected to the pelvis, will travel an arc that brings it higher, lifting the body upward as well as it does so, creating the "rise" of the rising trot on its own.

Another useful image, which adds the idea of controlling your horse's trot tempo with your posting, is to think of your thigh bone and knee as the swinging arm of a metronome (fig. 9). The tip of the arm of the metronome, where your hip joint would be, must rise as the metronome arm sweeps forward; no thought or energy need be spent on lifting the arm.

When you post correctly, your weight should continue to flow down the horse's sides throughout the posting sequence; try not to place more weight in the stirrups when you rise. At the same time, don't clench with your knees. Keep your torso quiet as your thighs lever your pelvic region upward and forward, and then back down to the saddle. Let your horse's natural movement give you the cue for the timing and sweep of your metronome. To strengthen the muscles needed to post and check that you are balanced correctly, a useful exercise is holding yourself at the top of the post for several strides, using your thigh and core muscles to keep you balanced over the horse, while your shoulders and upper body remain relaxed.

Veni Vidi Vici

Caesar reportedly wrote this sentence—"I came, I saw, I conquered"—to describe his defeat of Pharnaces II of Pontus at the battle of Zela. For him, it was simply a matter of showing up and looking at what he wanted in order to conquer it. When we ride, most of us stare at our horse's head as if it is the horse we wish to conquer, instead of the path ahead. Instructors nag us to look up, but they don't tell us what to do with our gaze. With nothing else to do, we invariably drop our eyes back down to the horse's head. If we allow our body to feel our horse's body, however, we can actually use our eyes to prepare the road ahead by drawing an imaginary line in the sand for the horse to follow.

Let's take a look at how to use this in riding the corners between M and C and then C and H on the left rein. As you approach M, look over to C and draw a line in the sand from C back to M. To draw this line you must calculate how deep into the corner you and your horse can handle at that moment. Not as an ideal, mind you, but what the two of you can handle at that one instance. As you pass through M, set your horse onto this line of travel and again look over to C and draw the line again back to you as you are riding. This will strengthen your line and help you to better stay the course you have set. As you then approach C, look over to H and now draw a line from H back to C. Again, calculate what corner you and your horse can handle to determine your line, and as you begin to ride through C, look again over to H and draw the line again. Think of it as your eyes almost pulling your horse along, or even as placing your horse at H and then riding him to where he already is, waiting for you.

To ride a circle in this manner, divide the circle into four arcs and use your eyes to draw lines through them. To traverse a diagonal from, say, F to H, draw a line with your eyes from H back to F, but then find X on this line and draw a line back to you from X. As you approach X, find H again and repeatedly draw your line back to you from there.

Once you have begun drawing lines with your eyes at home, it is time to turn on your internal camcorder. Later in the day or in the evening before going to sleep, try playing back your ride in your mind. Don't envision an illustration of a dressage arena from above with you as a dot moving through the patterns. Put yourself back in the saddle and turn on your internal camcorder to play back your ride in the actual arena you ride in. If the barn is over there by E, or a certain plant or tree is near H, include that in your playback. Allow your mind's eye to see the sweep around a corner, the extent of the long side, and so on. When you next return to the arena in real life, check your video playback for its accuracy and edit as necessary. Now your eyes are drawing your path forward and taking in wider surroundings. When you then go to a show, layer this video image of your ride at home onto the foreign and perhaps slightly scary show ring. You've just made the show ring more comfortable and given yourself some extra signposts to help you in your ride.

Quick Taps and Steady Pressure—The Driving Leg Aids

It was a beautiful, clear day, perfect for a school fair. The sun was out and shining, and even though summer was fast approaching, its heat hadn't yet arrived. Kids were squealing in delight, running from one event or game to another, with butterflies or flowers painted on their faces, often also smeared with cotton candy, as parents trailed behind, or mingled around benches and picnic tables. But the line that followed the contours of an impromptu tape fence for a distance and then turned and snaked through a number of obstacles was for one of the big events, the pony ride.

There were four ponies working. As each excited child was fitted with a helmet, the parents moved off for a good view to start snapping away. The horses were of different colors and shapes, as were the children; each ride was unique to each child and parent. But there was an eye-opening similarity for those of us trying to learn how to create proper connections between our bodies and the horse's circle of muscles. To get her pony to move off, each child looked down at his head, hopped up and down in the saddle, and shook the reins in her hands. The ponies nonchalantly accepted this flurry of activity and then quietly moved forward when the handler began walking. Why do we all do this? What is it that makes us think shaking the reins is a logical thing to do to make a horse move? Our instinct, the ingrained human nature, of course, is to use our eyes, our upper bodies, and our hands to do things. We mold with our hands, our tools have handles, we use straps to hang things from our shoulders. So it is only natural that the children that day at the fair would all use the same technique to get their mounts moving.

Soon, we learn not to hop up and down, managing to use our leg without so much movement in our body. Then we concentrate on keeping our hands "quiet." But unfortunately, most of the time we are merely taught to stifle the symptoms of incorrect fundamentals—what we look like while riding—leading to blocks and tightness in our bodies. Instead, we must change the fundamentals themselves, redirecting the movement and energy in our bodies. Jumping up and down and shaking the reins is not bad because it is ugly to look at, though it is, but because it is essentially ineffective and harmful to the horse.

At this point, many readers are probably saying to themselves, "Yes, but that is a kid thing. Most adults do not do that. I certainly don't." What I would like for you to entertain is that in fact you do, just to a slightly more subtle degree. There are few fundamentals to dressage technique, but the few that exist influence everything we do on a horse. And the ways in which we stray from these fundamentals are countless and ever-present because of the way we as humans are programmed to interact with our surroundings. To flow with the horse, plug into his back, and influence his circle of muscles through riding back to front are, on the face of them, easy concepts to grasp. But riding will include frequent epiphanies where we realize yet again how something we have been doing all along contributes to riding front to back. Each "Oh, now I get it!" will be followed in time by another "Oh, now I get it!" which will in turn be followed by an "Oh, now I really get it!" and so on.

The legs and seat drive a horse forward, not the hands, nor the arms, nor the upper body. Instead of learning the fundamentals of back-to-front riding, we are first taught instead to stop shaking our reins and to keep our hands "quiet." So the instinct to move our hands gets pushed back up our arms to our shoulders, where we become tight. Now, every time we ask a horse to move off, we tighten our shoulders and lean forward. The instinct has not been addressed. We still want to "shake the reins" long after we believe we have progressed far beyond those children riding at the school fair.

Let's review, then, the basic driving leg aids. You have probably heard of the driving seat, and there is a great deal you will be able to do with the tilting of your pelvis and weighting a seat bone, but for now, at training level, let us just concentrate on our lower legs. Generally, there are two ways to use our legs, by pressing our leg against the horse or by giving him a succinct tap or kick with our foot. To teach our horse to become sensitive to the leg aids, and later the seat aids, we may first need to start with this later tap or kick aid to ask our horse to move off. It is important to give this aid only once and then relax and let your horse respond to it.

If he doesn't respond to this, then give the aid again a little stronger or with a tap of the whip at the same time. When he then responds, praise him. Teach the horse to respond to this leg aid; don't let him teach you to ineffectually kick him every stride around the arena. If he is moving forward, don't kick. This is very easy to understand, but it is frustratingly difficult to change when you have fallen into bad habits. When the horse knows that a quick tap or kick means forward, you may then use this aid to encourage him forward if he slows or hesitates.

At training level, it is enough to work simply on the ability to give this simple kick aid without popping out of the saddle, tightening your upper body, leaning forward, or moving your hands. It will be much harder than you think, and you will thank yourself later for taking the time on this now. Remember, as riders we are managing the flow in our bodies and directing it without creating blocks elsewhere. Do not belittle this. It is a much more complicated and satisfying skill than simply kicking our horse around the arena, and you will need to take some time and effort to learn it.

When we have learned to use our leg independently from our seat, we will be able to work on the full leg pressure aid.

Corridors, Force Fields, and Cowboys and Indians—The Molding Leg Aids

Three images are helpful when using the molding leg aids. As you ride a circle, for example, imagine that you are riding down the center of a curved corridor. If the horse begins to veer out of the circle, he will hit the outside wall of the corridor and bounce back into the middle; if he starts to fall into the middle of the circle, he will hit the inside wall and bounce back into the middle. The power of this corridor image is that it is not simply a metaphor. Your legs and reins are actually physical barriers that you use to keep your horse on track.

For the second image, remember the plastic cowboy and Indian figures that you might have played with when you were young. Some of these figures, made of hard plastic in bright primary colors, were molded bow-legged with their arms out in front of them in an eternal riding position. Little peg protrusions stuck out at their calves, which matched holes on each flank of the matching little plastic horses, allowing you to snap the figure onto the horse. When riding the corridor, think of being the yellow plastic Indian or cowboy whose inflexible legs and arms are the walls of the corridor. The horse may waffle a little at first between these walls, but will stabilize as you bring the walls in closer. The plastic Indian image also reminds us to open our pelvis and relax our inner thigh muscles, which tend to pinch us out of the saddle when flexed, and instead use our outside thigh muscles to keep our legs toned, while opening our seat to allow the horse's motion to pass through and over his back. This image is especially useful for riders who have low natural muscle tone and might be a little too floppy on a horse; it is less useful for a rider who might already tend to be tense and rigid.

The third image is that of the force field ubiquitous in science-fiction films. These force fields are invisible until the unsuspecting character walks into one. Suddenly, a wall of electric blue squiggles appears, throwing the character back a few yards. Just as quickly, it becomes invisible again. Think of your legs as this force field: they are quiet and invisible at rest, but when the horse tries to shove against one, it activates to keep him aligned. Just as quickly, having done its work, it returns to its quiet, invisible state.

It may now be apparent that the molding aids are our steering aids. We use our seat and legs to drive the horse forward, to set a horse back or halt him, and also to steer. We do not use our hand and rein aids for this. The most important use of our rein aids is in encouraging the circle of muscles to work properly. And in order to establish this connection, we must first understand a little about bit contact.

Bit Contact

While the horse is on his way to rhythm and relaxation, the rider must also begin to establish his proper relationship to the bit; that is, to learn how to allow the horse to accept a regular and even contact. This is not to say that the rider should pull the horse's head in with his hands, trying to put the horse's head "on the vertical" and the horse "on the bit." Sadly, many riders can be seen at shows with their horse's necks straight out and their heads tucked down onto the vertical, so that the whole image is of a sideways 7. This outline comes from placing too much emphasis on the horse's head position without understanding that this position is merely a byproduct of correct movement, not an end in itself. When we realize how important it is that the horse be allowed to raise his withers and the base of his neck, we can understand how forcing his nose in and down in a false "head set" can negatively affect the engagement of his hindquarters. This merely traps him onto his forehand and adds stress and tension to his neck, back, and hind legs.

Since we desire the horse to be on the aids and not simply "on the bit," we must first engage the horse's hind end; in other words, first start the motor. When the horse is pushing off effectively from behind, we can then feel the movement over his back and into the top of his neck. Whatever force we generate from behind will have to be dealt with up front in our hands. It is important at this point to stress that we should never pull back on the reins. All dressage riding is concerned with forward movement and thought. We may bring our inside hand to the side to act as a leading direct rein; we may also give our hands forward to reward the horse or encourage him to stretch and seek the bit; but we must never pull back.

Most of us rely too heavily on our hands to "control" the horse. By developing her core muscles, the rider acquires the important ability to ride from her seat. This will also give her confidence that she can slow or halt the horse from her seat, and thus use her hands to influence, rather than rigidly control, allowing the horse's neck the freedom it needs to move properly.

When we first engage the hind end, we generate a force that comes up over the horse's back, a force we can feel in our hands. It is our responsibility to receive this force; that is, to accept the contact and the weight as we ask a horse to assume a frame. At this point we may need to help him along in this new frame that we ask of him until he develops the muscle, balance, coordination, and mental ability to handle it on his own. "Handling it on his own" is what we mean when we talk of "self-carriage." The toggle between being on the aids and being in self-carriage is never-ending. We ask for a frame, a degree of balance; we help the horse to achieve this balance by allowing a little more weight in our hands; he then, by building his muscle and coordination, becomes lighter in the bit as his balance is shifted; meanwhile we move on to the next stage, asking him for a higher degree of balance that we will again need to help him with, and so on.

As long as we remember that we are not pulling back on the reins, but that the weight we feel in our hands comes from the push from behind, and that we are simply receiving this weight without letting it shoot out of the horse's brow like a fountain, we can then convince ourselves not to shy away from this contact, this weight. The weight in our hands is equal to the power from behind. If we do not hold this force in our hands, then the power spills out of the horse's front end; if we take more weight in our hands than is generated from behind, then we are actually pulling back and working against the push from behind. We turn on a fire hose of energy from behind that pulses over the horse's back and over the top of his neck, but we cannot let it continue to shoot out of his head. We must contain it.

Once we have the horse moving and desire him to be on the aids, we must understand that there will be a moment of tension as the power we generate from behind comes up into our hands. If we let go of this new power because we are uncomfortable with the tension that we have just generated, the horse will likely be flat and rushy. If, on the other hand, we have faith that the horse will come to us and assume the responsibility of accepting this request for a balance, the horse will reward us by giving himself to us. The tension builds, as if in a pressure cooker, and then, as if a switch has been flipped, the horse accepts the request, the pressure is released, he softens in the bridle, and his back begins to rise. Suddenly we feel a great release in our hands. When this happens we respond in kind by giving our hands forward. We only need to give the slightest bit, just a fraction of an inch forward, for the horse to feel and understand this reward. Giving too much risks losing the equilibrium we have only just established.

When the horse is asked to come through from behind, and when he meets the passive resistance of our hands that causes him to relax into an improved balance, then we have the beginnings of the horse being on the aids. Remember that the area in front of the horse's withers should remain relaxed, with no wrinkles, and his neck should reach outward in an arc, with the horse's head in front of the vertical. As the horse continues in his training and in the development of his frame, his head will come in and up, but only because the muscles of the neck and shoulder are being properly worked and strengthened and because he is taking more weight on his haunches. From now on, we take on the responsibility of constantly fine-tuning and adjusting this relationship between our driving leg and our receiving hand.

Once we understand connection, we must understand just how much weight or contact to have in our hands; we still need to develop a sense of the correct feeling in the reins. But what is this correct feeling? As is so often the case with riding, the correct feeling lies somewhere in the subtle middle of things, not too much contact and not too little.

Think of tuning a stringed instrument. As you pluck the string, you tighten and loosen the string until you begin to zero in on your target. Let's say that you are attempting a G. As you get closer to the G, you will begin by overs- and undershooting it, so that you start to hear an A-flat, then an F-sharp. Soon it wavers between a G-sharp and a G-flat, and finally you arrive at G. Just as you must hear both sides of the note before finding it exactly, you must also be willing to feel what we might call both sides of contact to appreciate what is too hard and what is too soft.

It is quite possible that the same rider can have differing contacts in different gaits—too little at the trot and too much at the canter, for example. But for the sake of simplicity and clarity, think of a rider having either too little or too much contact. The rider with too little contact allows the reins to sag continually, or to flop and tighten repeatedly. Such a rider often cannot develop a strong enough seat to keep the horse forward with some contact. The rider who is hesitant to take a contact also risks repeatedly jerking the horse in the mouth with the bit, though she may think she is kinder to the horse when she does not take a strong contact. Because there is no support for the suspension bridge necessary to raise the horse's back and strengthen him to carry the rider, the horse will travel hollow, with his hind legs trailing, and more often than not develop a large muscle on the underside of his neck, so that he moves more like a turkey than a horse.

The rider who takes too much contact, on the other hand, will have short, taut reins. The horse's neck will be tense and contracted in front of the withers, often showing wrinkles there, and his head will be cranked in with his throatlatch closed. And just as with too little contact, instead of proper muscling along the top of his neck, he will develop a bulge underneath. Since the horse is pulled in at the front by the tight contact, you will again see a hollow back and a weak hind, as the rider's strong hands prevent his hind legs from reaching underneath him.

On the Way to the Half-Halt

The half-halt is a deceptively simple idea that nonetheless requires a sensitive and complicated combination of aids and timing. The basic principle is the shifting of the flow of the horse upward and of his balance back toward his haunches, and can be applied to all gaits. The two aspects of the half-halt are the driving aids of the leg and seat and the receiving and molding aids of the rider's hands. These two parts can be further divided into the left and right driving aids and the left and right receiving aids, so that all told there are four aids that can be used separately or in various combinations to effect a variety of half-halts, directing energy through different parts of the horse's body. However, though there is a world of nuanced aid combinations and timing to the half-halt, at this point let's just stay out of the weeds a while and focus on an easier, more general approach.

The rider, through her position and relaxation, connects the flow of movement in her body to that of the horse and, by doing this, is then able to control this flow of movement, or energy. Instead of riding the "proper" half-halt that drives with the seat, at this point it is best to think of using your seat as an abrupt block and release of this movement of the horse. The mechanics of this half-halt will vary slightly depending on the gait and whether you are posting or sitting to the trot, but the general effect will be the same, almost as if you took a quick still photo from a segment of video and immediately returned it to the flow.

At training level, you will use your half-halt most just before a change in gait or direction, or as a correction for when your horse rushes. Simply put, it will act as an attention grabber or "pause aid."

Imagine that you've seen a friend walking along on the other side of the street, and you want to get his attention so you can wave to him. If you call out to him, you will get his attention, but you will also notice a certain amount of pause or hesitation in his stride. After a stride or two he may even stop, if you continue to wave. Now that you have his attention, you will be able to ask him to wait up for you or to cross the street over to your side himself. In the same way, when a horse stops paying attention to you and begins to rush, you will need to get his attention back again, and in doing this you will also create a physical halt or pause while his attention is drawn away from his own world. Once you have his attention, you can now ask him to slow down, for example, so that your seat can catch up with him or he can come over to your side of the street.

Now imagine that you and a friend are walking along together, and suddenly you cry out, "Run!" and immediately set off. Obviously your friend will be too surprised to start running right at the same time and will find herself a few paces behind you. If, instead, you were walking along together and you said, "Look, I have an idea. At that mailbox up there, let's start running," both of you would be prepared; and when the two of you did make it to the mailbox and you cried out, "Now, run!" both of you would be able to take off at the same time. This is exactly what will happen when you half-halt your horse to alert him to an upcoming change in direction or gait.

Again, to understand when to half-halt is to feel the movement of the horse and your body's connection to it. At the walk, the rider simply checks for a split second and then releases the forward motion of her hips caused by the forward push from the horse's hind legs. This in turn checks the horse's movement and releases it again. In the posting trot, again the rider checks her forward phase of her post. And at the canter, she draws her hips back more forcefully at the 3 phase of the 1-2-3 count of the canter.

The "checking" of the hips is performed with a quick tightening and releasing of the abdominal muscles. So again, in the walk, the rider sinks her seat in the split second that she pulls back her hips. In the posting trot, just a centimeter before finishing the forward thrust of the post, the rider uses her core to forcefully check her hips and draw back slightly before resuming the usual smooth return to the seat. And at the canter, she uses her core to more forcefully draw her hips back in the 3 phase of the 1-2-3 count of the canter. At all gaits a quick squeeze and release of the fingers can match the checking phase of the rider's seat.

The Release of the Aid Is the Aid

This brings us to one of the golden rules of riding. The desired result of any aid is directly related to, and in fact accomplished by, the release of that aid. Keep it always in your mind that the release of the aid is in fact the aid itself. In the case of the half-halt, it is imperative that at the moment that you check your hips, you release them again. To effectively use the aid, you must have in your mind, even before executing the aid, its release.

Asking and Receiving

Inherent in the formula "The release of the aid is the aid" is having the patience to wait for your horse to respond. When you are not riding a test, take the time to prepare yourself for a movement, then give your horse a heads-up; only after this, execute the aid for the movement itself. If you wish to trot off from the walk, for example, go over in your mind how you will ask the horse for the trot, what aids you will use; and at the same time prepare him physically by positioning him for the transition with a half-halt so that he is also mentally prepared. Then give the aid for trot and immediately release; don't wait for the trot before releasing the trot aid. The trot will come with its release. In other words, ask for the trot and then allow the horse to respond by giving you the trot. Don't nag him into it. If he does not respond to the aid, then that is his mistake. You cannot cover for him, if you hope for him to learn. Let him make the mistake, get his attention, ask again, and praise him when he responds. In this way, you will set up a situation where the horse learns and is praised for learning. And with all learning, the key is to create a desire and an enjoyment in the process of learning. Simply put, better to teach with the carrot than the stick.

The Training Level Frame

Sooner or later you will be confronted with the idea of an overall frame for your horse. As the word implies, the interest here is in the horse's outline or silhouette. As the horse progresses in his athletic ability, this outline or silhouette will change. What is quickly apparent to most of us is the elevation of the horse's head and the amount of arch in his neck. What is less actively looked for, if noticed at all, is the amount of articulation in the hind joints and the lowering of the horse's croup.

Elsewhere in this book we have talked about the danger of using a helpful hint or sign as if it were the desired goal. Our goal is not to get the horse's head just in front of the vertical, for example; our goal is to ask the horse to work properly, and as he gains in strength and balance we will find that his head comes naturally toward the vertical.

Unfortunately, the concept of frame carries with it a similar danger. The horse's frame is a result of his balance. As his balance shifts from his forehand to his hind, his head will rise, his neck will arch, his hind joints will articulate, and so on. One of the clues, therefore, that we may look for in evaluating a horse's balance is this outline, silhouette, or frame.

Problems, however, arise when we look only at part of this outline. Since most of us tend to look predominantly at a horse's head and neck, it is tempting to simply pull the horse's head and neck in to match that silhouette in our mind. This is known as absolute elevation. As the horse develops his muscles and is encouraged to take more weight on his hind end, his front end will come up as a result of this, and display relative elevation, which looks at the relationship between a lifted forehand and a lowered hind end. When we look only for absolute elevation, we fail to understand the proper cause, that the horse is balanced more on his hind end.

Balance and musculature create the horse's frame. Instead of trying to put your horse into a training or first level frame, think instead of helping him gain muscle and improve his balance. If he has the muscle and balance to trot in a twenty-meter circle or to go somewhat into the corners, try asking for a slightly smaller circle or to go deeper into those corners. Always be aware of what he is capable of, what he can do with a little bit of extra effort, and what would overface him.

The Road Ahead

Take the time to secure your seat by strengthening your core muscles and allowing your rein and leg aids to be independent, which will allow you to have a correct and sympathetic bit contact. Learn the physiology of the horse, so that you better understand how to influence him in a way that is easy and comfortable for him. Appreciate how the horse's movement and attitude reflect your own. If you relax, he will too. If you are light with your hands, he will be light in the bridle. If you strengthen your core muscles and lengthen the back of your neck, he will raise his back and use his neck properly. And you may even find that if you ride with a clenched jaw, he will be dry and insensitive in his mouth.

Studies using a saddle scanner have shown that a well-balanced heavier rider stresses the horse's back less than a stiff, unbalanced lightweight rider; it is not your weight but your balance that most affects the horse. So take the time now to ride the basic movements properly and beautifully; the two of you will then be all the more able to handle the movements that follow.

Don't think of snapshots or still photos when contemplating your riding. You and your horse are constantly moving through space and time; opening up your mind to the changes that both of you are going through will help you to be a better rider in each ride, as well as to know when it is time to work on a movement and when it is time to push your horse along to the next step in the training process.

Finally, never take yourself out of the picture. Just as you apply the concepts of the pyramid to training your horse, apply them also to yourself. Take the time to condition both your body and your mind, developing a balanced seat and an awareness of your horse and surroundings. Try to include both you and your horse when you evaluate a situation; say, for example, "We are having trouble with the right lead canter," "I'm not sure how to get him to relax in the trot," or "I think we've got our twenty-meter circles down," rather than "He has trouble with the right lead canter," "He won't relax in the trot," or "He can do a nice twenty-meter circle."

Above all, have patience. There will be many periods when your body just won't do what you want it to, or when you feel as if everything should be going well, but it just isn't. These are frustrating times, and you will have your fair share of them. But through it all, remember that you are the leader and thus the one who takes full responsibility. Give your horse the benefit of the doubt and treat him with patience and kindness; give him the chance to come to you, to follow your lead. The horse is such a powerful, yet such a gentle, creature. If he allows you to sit on his back even for just a single stride, praise him. For he has just given you more than you will ever be able to give him in return.

Part 2

From the Judge's Box

The qualities that make up beautiful and correct riding are also those that are sought after and evaluated by judges at competitions, so it should come as no surprise that the general concerns and specific movements that first engage us are also those evaluated in the training level tests. Since the two worlds of correct riding and competitive riding are not only linked but overlap, understanding beautiful and correct riding helps us to understand how tests are scored at shows, and conversely, competition scores reflect the judge's skill in evaluating beautiful and correct riding. More specifically, the scores reflect the skill and training of a horse-and-rider pair, because it is through skill and training that they reach this beautiful and correct riding, not simply through the horse's natural movement. Though the judge's purpose is to evaluate training and to rank the entrants of each class in order, according to the training of both the horse and rider, the judge is not allowed to evaluate what she thinks a pair is capable of doing, or how they might normally perform a specific movement. The score must reflect only what the horse-and-rider pair have accomplished at that moment, in that class, on that day.

Show scores, then, can be seen in the light of training plus pressure. Your goal at a show is to ride the best test you can, but you will be up against psychological pressure as well as a myriad of outside influences that do not exist at home. Even if you and your horse master these outside distractions, there is no guarantee that you will accomplish your best at that particular moment. This can be of some solace if you have a bad ride. However, do not dismiss these disappointing rides; it is also true that we show our weaknesses precisely when we are under pressure, so these scores and judge's comments will be of great value in helping you understand yourself and your horse, even when you ride below what you believe is your norm.

Let's first get a better understanding of how a judge evaluates a test—what is called a judge's methodology—and then learn how to read a score sheet. (Note: All the vocabulary in this section relies on the definitions set down in the USDF Glossary of Judging Terms, available online.)

The Judge's Methodology: B + C +/- m = S

The underlying guiding principal for dressage judging is the correct biomechanics of the horse and rider. A horse that moves beautifully is a horse that moves in keeping with its innate biomechanics, and dressage is the proper gymnasticizing of the horse with this in mind. The correct use of biomechanics is referred to as the basics, and is represented by the B in the above formula. When a horse and rider perform a movement, the first thing the judge checks are the basics; that is, did the horse perform this movement with a clear rhythm and the correct amount of impulsion and submission? While the horse's gaits must be clear at any level of training, the judge's expectations for a horse's impulsion and submission increase as the horse goes up through the levels. This is because the judge is constantly checking to see if the horse has sufficient impulsion and submission to perform each movement. It follows, then, that a greater amount of impulsion and submission is needed, and therefore expected, to perform passage then a twenty-meter circle at the working trot. This ability of the horse sets the base score for the movement.

The second part of our formula, the C, refers to the criteria of the movement; that is, did the horse perform the movement? The horse may have lovely basics, but if the twenty-meter trot circle ends up looking more like an oval, the criteria of the movement is being performed poorly. The horse may take the canter depart beautifully, but if the rider has asked for it too soon or too late, then the score must come down.

The last part of our formula is "+/- m," in which m refers to any modifiers that may influence the score. The common modifiers in training level include use of corners, shying, stumbling, inattention, and nonessential parts of the movement. For example, if a judge was trying to decide between a 6.5 or a 7 for the first halt at X, she could consider the entrance at A and the trot from X to C. If those parts of the movement were accurate and well ridden, she would feel comfortable and happy with giving that movement a 7. If, on the other hand, the horse wandered a little on the centerline or shied slightly after X, she would unhappily go with the lower score of 6.5.

Now that we have a better understanding of how a judge formulates the scores, let's take a look at a score sheet.

The Score Sheet

In the title box of a USEF training level score sheet, along with the explanations of the conditions, a note to the reader, and a brief note on the trot work and the halt, the purpose of the training level tests is given. As it is so fundamental to an understanding of the training level tests, I will repeat it here: "To confirm that the horse is supple and moves freely forward in a clear and steady rhythm, accepting contact with the bit." This is a somewhat more biomechanical wording of the first two steps of the training pyramid, rhythm and relaxation. "Accepting contact with the bit" means that the horse has a positive relationship to the idea of the bit and that he doesn't shy from it. He need not maintain consistent contact with the bit at this point. Always keep the purpose of training level in mind when training and riding the tests.

The bulk of the score sheet is divided into two sections, the movements and the collectives. Below these two sections is a space for further remarks from the judge. This section is not part of the scoring of the test, but simply a place for the judge to add any comments that she may find useful, encouraging, or important.

All scores are given as a number from 0 to 10. Below is the exact meaning and explanation of each mark.

10: Excellent
9: Very good
8: Good
7: Fairly good
6: Satisfactory
5: Sufficient
4: Insufficient
3: Fairly bad
2: Bad
1: Very bad
0: Not executed

The top three scores show extra quality in basics, on top of correctly fulfilling the criteria of the movement. The next two (6 and 7) show that the horse and rider pair are on the right track with both basics and criteria. The 5 score shows only marginal execution. A 4 means that there is at least one major problem in basics or criteria. The scores 1 through 3 are given for serious or multiple problems with performance in basics, criteria, or both.

The Movements

The way you and your horse perform a specific movement is evaluated in the movements section of the test. Reading across the first row shows us first where a certain movement is expected to happen, then what that movement is, followed by the "directive ideas," or the qualities of that movement that the judge will be weighing when evaluating your performance. The next three boxes include the score, any possible modification of that score in the way of coefficients, and the final total for that movement. In each test, a number of movements will be considered important enough to warrant an enhancement of that score. Thus a movement with a coefficient of 2 will be doubled. A further modification of these scores can be made in the way of penalties for, say, going off course or leaving out a movement. The final box of the row allows the judge to give more specific remarks to clarify that movement's score.

Each movement in the first section of the score sheet is scored separately. Only what happens in that movement is evaluated for that movement by the judge, so that if something goes wrong in one movement, it will not be included in the evaluation of the next movement. Remember this while riding the test. If you ride one movement poorly, or if the horse shies during a movement, it will only affect the score for that one movement. Keep your concentration, move on, and ride the best you can for the remaining movements of the test.

Each movement is given a single score. However, since many movements include several aspects, the judge will give more weight to what is called the essence of each movement. For example, the very first movement of each training level test is: "Enter at A at working trot, halt at X, salute, proceed working trot." The essence of this movement is the halt at X, though the transition in and out of the halt, and the trot before and after, will inform the final score.

The Collective Marks

The collective marks section allows the judge to evaluate you and your horse's ability in the basics, the building blocks of good riding: gaits, impulsion, submission, and the rider's score. Though they are not clearly presented as such on the score sheet, and the last is even entitled Harmony, the last three collective marks are meant to be considered as rider scores. To highlight the importance of training, the gait score is only given a coefficient of one, while the impulsion and submission scores are given a coefficient of two, and the combined rider score has a coefficient of three.

Gaits (freedom and regularity)

The first item listed in the collective marks section is "Gaits," with a parenthetical qualifier of "freedom and regularity." In other words, a judge looks at these two qualities, the freedom of movement and the regularity of the footfall, to evaluate the horse's gaits.

The freedom of a horse's gait refers to the reach, scope, and lack of constriction in the movement of the fore and hind limbs. Reach refers to the length of step forward of the horse's legs, their forward extension. At higher levels, this would inform the range of stride lengths that a horse may have between lengthened, medium, or extended gaits on the one hand and collected gaits on the other, but at training level we are looking more at a baseline movement. Scope refers to what is called the amplitude of the movement. This also includes reach, but adds the idea of roundness in the stride; that is, how high the horse's hooves actually come up from the ground. And finally, constricted movement is limited either by external restraint, by forceful shortening, or by sustained muscular contraction.

Regularity concerns the purity of the gait; that is, the correct order and timing of the footfalls and phases of a gait. It evaluates whether the horse's rhythm is clean or not. The walk has a four-beat rhythm; that is, each of the four hooves lands separately. The trot has a two-beat rhythm;

the legs travel in diagonal pairs so that the near fore and off hind hooves land together, as do the off fore and near hind hooves. The canter has a three-beat rhythm. Here a front hoof lands alone, a diagonal pair lands together next, and finally by the lone hind hoof follows. The rhythm of a horse's gait, used in this sense, should not be confused with its tempo, which is the speed at which footfalls alternate, or the rate of repetition of a horse's stride.

A common example of an irregular gait is the lateral walk. In a clean walk, the hind hoof almost reaches the front hoof before the front hoof leaves the ground and starts moving forward. This means that we see a triangle (you might think of it as an upside-down triangle), with the horse's body making up the top horizontal line, the two legs marking the two other sides of the triangle, and the hooves creating the point at the bottom. A lateral walk will not create this triangle. An irregular walk might have only slight lateral tendencies, where the point of the triangle that the hooves should make becomes a little blurred or soft, or can be quite lateral (or "pacey"), with the front and hind legs moving together, so that the hind hoof always stays the same distance from the front foot, and never comes close to making a triangle.

The canter can also be lateral, but a more common irregularity is the four-beat canter. It is interesting to note that technically the canter does have four beats; there is a "silent" beat when all hooves are up off the ground. There was once a great debate as to whether the horse really did achieve this "unsupported transit," as it was then called, until the expatriate English photographer Eadweard Muybridge proved its existence with his zoopraxiscope (which many consider the first movie projector). When we talk today of the three beats of the canter, we mean those three beats we hear when the hooves are hitting the ground. If all four hooves hit the ground separately in the canter, we call this irregularity a four-beat canter.

Regularity, like freedom, involves the length and height of the horse's steps, but in this case it is in relation to each other. Thus, freedom has to do with the length and amplitude of motion of a horse's strides as a whole, but regularity compares the length and amplitude of the path taken by the right fore, say, and the left fore. This makes sense if you consider that a horse could not have a different length of stride from one front leg to the other, or pick up one hoof higher and therefore take longer to put it down again, without this changing its rhythm.

Finally, regularity is an indicator of soundness. Judges must be both diligent and extremely careful when assessing a horse's soundness. On the one hand, a judge must always be ready to stop a test for the sake of the horse's health and well-being. But on the other hand many horses have gait issues due to previous injuries, so that the horse's gait may be affected although it is no longer in any discomfort or danger, or may be blocked in its movement by the rider or by previous training. The judge, then, must first distinguish between an underlying soundness issue and a misstep, a momentary lack of balance, or shortness due to constraint.

A common rule of thumb in evaluating the soundness of a horse is whether a gait is irregular in both directions; another is whether a horse shows irregularity in two or more gaits. If a judge notices an irregularity in the trot to the left, for example, she would include that in her score for that movement. If the horse then shows an irregularity in the trot to the right, she must then decide whether to ring the horse out. In another case, a horse might seem stiff in the trot to the left, then show an irregularity in its gait in the trot to the right. The judge may then include these observations in her scoring for those two movements. If the horse then shows an irregularity in its canter in either direction, the judge will have to consider that a more basic soundness issue might be at play.

Impulsion (desire to move forward, elasticity of the steps, suppleness of the back, engagement of the hindquarters)

Simply put, impulsion is thrust. But let's look at a more precise definition of this term. Impulsion is the release of the energy stored by the engagement phase of the gait. This energy is transmitted through a back that is free from negative tension and is manifested in the horse's elastic, whole-body movement.

The engagement phase of the gait is the moment when the hind leg is bearing weight just before pushing off. So we define engagement as the increased flexion of the lumbosacral joint and the joints of the hind leg during the weight-bearing (support) phase of the stride, thus lowering the croup relative to the forehand. This is not the same as a horse picking its feet up so that the joints are flexed while the leg is in the air. This "hock action" is what is commonly seen in gaited horses and hackneys.

In order to have impulsion, then, you must first have engagement followed by suspension, the phase where the horse has no feet on the ground. Since there is no phase of suspension in the walk (or the piaffe, for that matter), there is no impulsion in the walk. Thus, technically, impulsion concerns only the gaits of trot and canter.

With this definition in mind we can better understand the descriptions in parentheses: desire to move forward, elasticity of the steps, suppleness of the back, engagement of the hindquarters.

Engagement of the hindquarters is the precursor to the suspension phase of impulsion. The quality of the suspension phase of a gait can be no better than the engagement phase that comes before it.

Suppleness of the back reflects the horse's ability to direct the power of the haunches through the rest of the horse. Suppleness refers to the range of motion of joints, not to muscles. Muscles may be elastic, but joints are supple. The horse's spine is a relatively rigid structure compared to that of humans and other animals. The one point where real movement can occur is at the lumbosacral joint, where the last lumbar spine vertebra joins onto the pelvic vertebrae. This is the "coupling joint," found about where the horse's pelvis connects to his spine. And it is the ability of this joint to bend that plays a great role in engagement and its release.

Elasticity of the steps reflects both the whole-body movement of the horse and the suspension phase. Elasticity is the ability or tendency to stretch and contract the musculature smoothly, giving the impression of stretchiness or springiness.

To better understand the desire to move forward, we must look at the original French from which it is translated. Because the USDF follows the French Fédération Equestre Internationale (FEI) standards, our score sheets are translations from the French. "Desire to move forward" is thus a translation of the original, *desire de se porter en avant*. A more precise translation would be "desire to carry itself forward." Once we see that the original includes this idea of carrying power, of engagement, we can then better understand its presence here under impulsion.

That impulsion is listed under the collective marks for a training level test may seem a little strange, because in the training pyramid impulsion is further up the scale, after rhythm, relaxation, and connection. Why would our horse's impulsion be judged when only the very rudiments of connection, which comes before impulsion in the training pyramid, are expected?

The German pyramid of training lists *Schwung* as the fourth step of the pyramid. For the purpose of the training pyramid, this term is translated as "impulsion." Now, as a horse develops his strength and balance, he increases his impulsion. Impulsion is not a static quality, but one that increases through training. When we talk of impulsion in relation to the training pyramid, we are dealing with a greater amount of impulsion than what is needed for a training level test. The impulsion listed in the training pyramid is the level of impulsion necessary for the medium and extended gaits, which of course only begin to appear at second level. A trainer, therefore, would probably not talk of impulsion with a training level horse, but a judge will be evaluating the beginnings of the continuous development of impulsion in the horse. The judge will not expect medium paces from a training level horse, but she will be checking to see if the horse is moving freely forward, as required in the statement of purpose for the training level tests.

Submission (attention and confidence, lightness and ease of movements, acceptance of the bridle, lightness of the forehand)
Submission covers the horse's compliance and acceptance of the aids, and refers to both the horse's mental attitude and his physical state. A more complete definition can be found in the USDF's 2011 Glossary of Judging Terms: "The yielding of the horse's will to that of the rider, as revealed by a constant attention and confidence in the attitude of the horse, as well as by the harmony with the rider and willingness to: 1. perform the required exercise, and 2. operate with correct basics."

An easy starting point is to think of everything going on behind the saddle as concerning impulsion, while what goes on in front of the saddle has to do with submission. This is not a hard and fast rule; a horse that kicks out at a leg aid is still thought to have a submission problem, for example, even though the horse's kick takes place behind the saddle. But it does give us a good general framework when we are evaluating a horse. With this in mind, let's take a closer look at the parentheticals.

When the horse's ears are out to the side, this is one sign that the horse is attending to the rider, and by paying attention to the rider, he submits to the rider's lead within a partnership. And a confident horse performs with a boldness and self-assurance that comes with a trust in this partnership with his rider.

Horses are herd animals and take comfort in knowing where they stand in the herd hierarchy. If a horse feels that his rider has earned his trust, his submission, he will be a more content horse. If the rider leads with grace and understanding, guiding the horse with authority and establishing proper boundaries, the horse will respond with a confidence that stems from his acceptance of and submission to these boundaries. Simply put, if the rider is kind, confident, and happy, the horse will respond in kind and follow the rider's lead. And when he does, he will do so with a lightness and ease of movement.

If a rider is harsh with her hands and causes discomfort or pain to the horse's mouth, this of course would be recognized as a rider problem and no fault of the horse's. But there are times when the horse displays his bad attitude through picking a fight with the bit—rooting, tossing his head, opening his mouth, backing off the bit, and so on. Here the horse is stating clearly that he rejects the partnership, that he does not agree with the situation, that he does not submit to the rider.

It is important to note that the horse could very well have a point. Perhaps the rider has mistreated him in the past, maybe previous improper training has soured him, maybe it is simply that his tack does not fit and is causing him discomfort. The judge can only evaluate what she sees in that test on that day, however; all else is only conjecture and cannot be a part of her evaluation.

So the submission score is not a value judgment; it is simply an evaluation of the extent of the partnership between the horse and rider during the test. Perhaps the horse was spooked by something just before entering the ring, and the rider had no time to calm him before entering or completing the test. Perhaps the horse and rider have never met before the day of the test, so that any bad attitude on the part of the horse has nothing to do with the rider. The point is that there are many reasons why a partnership may be stressed during a test, but the judge can only judge what she sees.

As for lightness of the forehand being a factor in the submission score, let us consider a horse's attitude in the ring. Obviously, a horse that fights its rider, tosses its head, whips its tail, kicks out at leg aids, refuses, spooks, is constantly looking around at things outside the arena, and so on has a submission problem. But a horse that mopes around the arena, drooping his head and leaning on his shoulders, is also not displaying the best submission. Both throwing a tantrum and pouting are ways that the horse communicates that he is not submitting to his rider.

Rider (position and seat, correct and effective use of the aids, harmony between horse and rider)

Rider's position and seat. If a judge were to comment, "Elegant but ineffectual," the rider would at least know that, if nothing else, she will probably have a good position and seat score. The position and seat score evaluates the rider's posture and alignment, as well as her core strength and balance. It does not evaluate her use of her aids, nor their effect on the horse. The judge here will be looking for equal leg length on each side of the horse, the rider's seat in the middle of the saddle as viewed from behind, an upright posture, head on top of shoulders, and the general shoulder-hip-heel alignment. Sitting to one side, pitching forward, slumping back, teetering and sliding about, and so on will negatively affect this score.

Rider's correct and effective use of the aids. While there may be some discussion on more subtle uses of the aids, such as whether to focus on dropping the seat bone or putting the outside leg back for a canter depart, we can assume a general agreement on the correct use of the aids. A rider should not shake the reins to ask the horse to walk forward, she should not rise to the canter, and so on. And though a rider may give the horse a leg aid to ask him to move forward, excessive use of force of the leg and hand aids is harmful to the horse and will be penalized severely. It is the rider's responsibility to seek help from qualified instructors to learn the correct use of the aids.

But even if we use the aids correctly, we may not use them effectively. So this score also reflects the judge's evaluation of the possible causes of a low/high impulsion or submission score. If the rider galvanizes an otherwise lazy horse, or successfully rides through a trouble spot, calms a horse, or instills a sense of confidence and security in him, this score will reflect that rider's ability. And if the rider is unable to do these things, the judge must consider how much this score should reflect that as well. Sometimes this will not drop a rider's score. A horse may be tense and show no submission throughout a test, for example, because a loose horse is prancing about the show grounds. Unfortunately, the judge will be forced to lower the horse's submission score, but if the judge feels the rider handled the bad situation with calmness and aplomb, the rider's score may actually go up.

Harmony between horse and rider. Dressage is the ongoing pursuit of obedience and harmony through careful physical and mental development and conditioning of the horse and rider. The more "through" a horse is—that is, the more freely it allows the rider's aids to go through its body as a whole, from back to front—the more willingly and harmoniously he will respond to the rider's aids, and the more skilled and mature a rider is, the more she will be able to command this calm willingness to bring about a harmony between horse and rider. But let it be said that the rider must always take responsibility for the ride. A well-schooled and through horse may be able to carry a coarse or unskilled rider through a test, but this does not create a harmony between horse and rider, just as no matter how skilled a rider is rumored to be, she must take the blame for a horse that shows a lack of throughness or conditioning.

Some Final Comments on Judging

As you are performing each movement of your test, your judge is doing a number of things. First, she is giving the score and her comments for the previous movement to the scribe. While she is doing this, she is also filling in the formula B + C +/- m to come up with your score for the movement you are performing—evaluating the basics, checking to see that the criteria of the movement were fulfilled, and adding or subtracting for any smaller bits of information. While you are then on to the next movement, she is trying to find the best way to explain this information in a few words that the scribe can write in the comments section. These words will need to be concise, given the time restraints and the ability of the scribe, but still informative to the rider. While she is doing this, she is of course evaluating your next movement. At the same time, she is answering any questions that the scribe may have about her comments and making sure that the scribe is keeping up and on the right movement, as well as that the rider is performing the correct movements of the test and hasn't gone off course. She is also evaluating the collective marks and thinking about what further comments she may want to include.

It takes a lot of time, energy, money, organizational skill, and a certain temperament to become even an L graduate, let alone a high-level judge. The people who go through this to become judges do so because they believe in the sport and enjoy it. They want you to have a good ride, they want you to score high, but they must remain true to the tenets of the judging process. Comments are meant to be helpful, even though a rider may feel the criticism.

And finally, remember that judges are human. Keep in mind what it must be like to sit for hours on end for an entire day or two or sometimes three in a row, watching ride after ride, keeping the scribe on track, and maintaining a sharp mind and keen focus on every test. Still, the more we understand about what the judge is looking for, the more we will be able to differentiate between an outright mistake and an unpalatable truth, and learn from the latter.

Part 3

Gymnastic Exercises for Horse and Rider

Straight lines, circles, diagonals; these are the essential patterns of the training level tests and the building blocks of all the tests to come. They are also the geometrical foundation for all good riding.

To ride these properly, keep your eyes up and look where you are going. When crossing the diagonal, focus on the letter across the arena and use it to help you keep your horse from wandering this way and that. Though the rail will help you with your straight lines, keep it always in your mind that you must free yourself from this crutch. Test yourself constantly by riding the center or quarter line to see just how straight you are moving. Have the entire circle you are about to ride already in your mind and find it ahead of time by picking out your four points of the circle and drawing your arcs.

The other major part of your basics is the transition between gaits. Remember to make these transitions a steady diet, and always prepare in advance and ride your transition consciously.

Below are some exercises that may help you and your horse find rhythm and relaxation, and help you on your way to connection. They also mirror the movements found in the training level tests. Obviously, each horse and rider pair has its own strengths and weaknesses that can only be addressed by working with a trainer. This set of exercises is just a general base to work from.

Much of this book addresses the mental and theoretical approach to riding: the correct posture, the proper aids, specific patterns to practice, and so on. These are important if you are to become a correct and effective rider. However, since they are based on a logical and natural cause and effect, it is not enough that you simply understand these concepts intellectually. You must also be able to feel the horse under you. In whatever way works best for her, the rider must encourage herself to focus on feeling the pushing power from each of her horse's hind legs, the raising or lowering of either of his shoulders, or the difference between tension or looseness in his back, withers, and poll.

Finally, how do we put all of this together into a plan? The best way, of course, is to get a trainer to help you; but not all of us live in an ideal world, and many must work without a trainer much of the time. That being the case, here is one way you might put a session together. Although I cannot possibly tell you how to tailor it exactly to you and your horse, it may give you some insight into how your trainer is hoping to help you.

First, warm your horse up in all three gaits. Perhaps start with some active walk around the arena in both directions, followed by the string of pearls exercise described in part 3. Then pick up a rising trot and go three times around the arena, change direction through the diagonal, and go three times around the arena on the other rein. After the trot work, pick up your canter in a corner of the arena and canter one twenty-meter circle. If you feel good about this, perhaps try to canter the entire arena, then return to the trot, change rein again, and pick up your other canter. Use your corners to help you set your horse up for a good canter depart. Again canter a twenty-meter circle and, if comfortable, continue around the arena once. Now come back to the trot, settle yourself and your horse, and ask for some stretch at the trot on a twenty-meter circle. After this, come to the walk, give him long reins, tell him he's a good boy, and while you give him a break, plan your day's ride.

Use each ride-in to evaluate your horse so that you will be better able to decide what you might want to work on in that session, or to confirm any progress that the two of you have made. For example, you may ask yourself, Did he seem to fall in or pivot on the circle to one side and blow out of the circle to the other? Were the transitions quick or slow? Did he throw his head? Did you lean forward ahead of the movement or fall behind? How well did you manage to keep the tempo? If the tempo was off, where? Did he speed up toward the barn and slow down away from it? Did he shy from any area of the arena? How was the canter depart? Did his haunches fall in on either rein? Did he overbend his neck, or jackknife, in either direction? Did he seem counterbent in either direction? Was it difficult to come back down to the trot? Did you feel pitched forward? Did he stop abruptly?

These questions should have already presented themselves during the ride-in, but now you have a few minutes to put all of this information together to help you decide what you want to work on. Certainly, there will be many, many things to work on, but try to pick just one or two things that stand out in your mind.

Maybe you felt that he seemed a little tight to the right at the trot, perhaps even a little counterbent. You could also have felt that the overall rhythm was off, and that you never got into a groove with your posting. To help him bend right, you must remember that you cannot simply bend him constantly to the right for thirty minutes; you must challenge him a little and then relieve the pressure. The figure eight exercise, then, is perfect for this, since it works both sides of the horse evenly.

But perhaps changing the bend every circle is doing terrible things to your balance and posting. After completing the figure eight portion of your ride and, again, asking for some stretching from your horse, then giving him a short break, pick up the trot around the whole arena. This time, just work on rhythm and your posting, concentrating on how your body moves with his. And remember to work in both directions.

Now you have completed a ride-in and worked on two exercises. Even though you weren't schooling the canter this session, you should still ride more canter than just in the warm-up. So after a short break from your trot work, pick up the canter in each direction. Start with a twenty-meter circle, and if you are comfortable, go long. If your horse wants to break or run away with you along the long side, you can always just ride half of the arena and use another twenty-meter circle to regain control.

Finally, ask for another few circles of stretch at the trot, and walk your horse off to cool him down. If possible, take him out on a small trail ride at the walk.

Now you have a structured framework for your riding sessions that includes walk, trot, canter, and stretching for every ride, but that is also flexible enough to allow you to focus on a specific aspect of your riding. You might decide in your next session, for example, to replace the figure eight and trot work around the entire arena with the infinity exercise for your trot work and the snowman exercise to school cleaner canter departs. Or match up the links and progressive loop exercises. As you progress and your horse gains strength, you may also want to extend your initial ride-in to include more trot and canter. Remember, this is all just one example of a framework that you can tailor to your particular situation. Ask your trainer to help you with a weekly plan and to decide on a proper plan for you and your horse.

It All Comes from the Seat

It is impossible to overemphasize the importance of riding back to front; that is, driving the horse forward with your seat and legs and receiving and controlling this energy with your hands. Before we get to the patterns, there is a little exercise to try that is great for giving the training level rider an understanding of how powerful the seat can be, as well as how the correct aids work with the natural movement of the horse. It's a powerful demonstration to those new to dressage of just how effective riding from the seat can be.

While your horse is walking down the centerline, with your body completely relaxed and your hips moving with the motion over your horse's back, simply sink your inside, let us say left, hip down and forward. Because your inside left hip is pushed a little forward, your right (outside) hip will automatically drop back so that your outside leg will fall on the back part of the girth. Don't pull it back as if you were going to ask for a canter; just know that it has moved back just a fraction on its own. As your inside hip and seat bone press down and forward, your inside leg will press against your horse, and he will turn to the left. If he begins to pivot, simply apply a little more inside leg. Now that he is turning and the inside leg is activating his inside hind leg, you can mold and shape the amount of turn with your outside leg. Notice that in this exercise you are not using your reins—or even your lower legs—at all!

Another way to appreciate the power of the seat is to simply walk along the rail and allow your seat to relax; let your hipbones sway with the movement over your horse's back. Now ask for a transition to halt by simply stopping the movement of your hips with your stomach muscles. The first few times you try this, you may need to finish the halt with a little restraint in the reins, but quite soon you will be able to halt your horse simply by using your seat.

These two very easy exercises should be the basis for your understanding of all three gaits, all up and down transitions, and the turning of the horse to both left and right. All of these movements are performed by the seat aids and only modified by the hands.

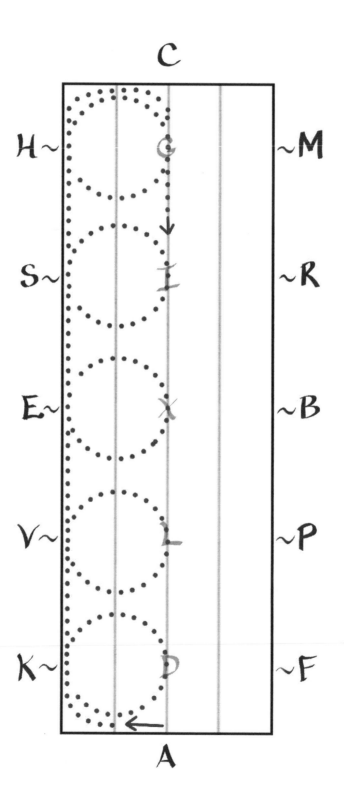

The String of Pearls

This is a suppling exercise done at the walk. Simply put, it is a succession of ten-meter circles along the long side, followed by a walk down the centerline to change direction.

Concentrate on using your leg and seat aids to hold the horse in position, so that your inside leg generates forward movement and blocks any tendency the horse may have to pivot or fall in on the circle. Your outside leg and outside rein mold the bend and keep the shoulder or haunches from bulging to the outside. Along the centerline, concentrate on keeping your horse straight. You may also practice a few walk-trot-walk transitions along the centerline.

Once you are comfortable steering your horse around these circles, you can challenge and improve your abilities and your horse's balance by advancing to what I call the Brussels Sprout pattern. Starting at A, walk up the centerline to D and then ride a ten-meter circle to the left toward K. When you return to the centerline again, ride up centerline to L; there, ride a ten-meter circle to the right toward P. Continue to alternate left and right circles in this way until you reach the far side of the arena. When you have mastered this, you can simply ride a series of small figure eights, so that when you come back from K to the centerline you simply turn right and ride a ten-meter circle toward F. Then ride up to L and ride another small figure eight, and so on.

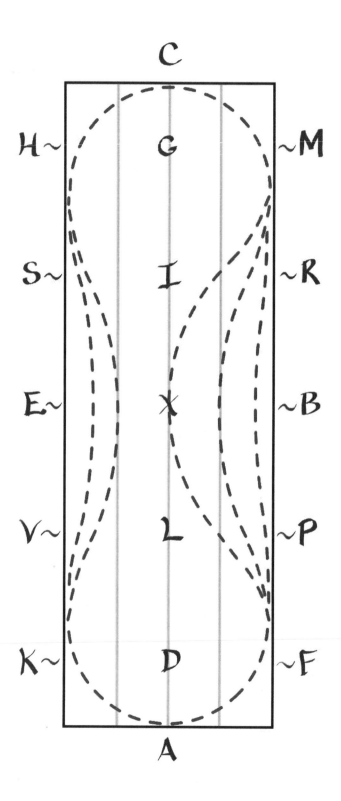

The Progressive Loop

This exercise prepares the horse and rider for the shallow loop in training level test 3. It progressively strengthens the horse's balance and the rider's ability to ask for and support a change of bend.

If we ride a loop from the rail to the centerline through X, the amount of bend in the horse is quite visible. If we ride a much shallower loop, curving from the rail to only a meter or two off the rail and back again, we become much more focused on and attentive to the aids that ask for this bend in the horse. Because we cannot rely as much on our eyes as when we follow a larger, more obvious curve, the very shallow loop challenges us to feel our horse and to concentrate on more subtle aids.

First, ride a shallow loop from the rail to the quarter line and back in both directions and determine how well you were able to support your horse and how well your horse kept his balance. Be attentive, also, to whether you could feel a difference between one direction and the other. If you feel that this is enough of a challenge for you both, then practice this loop a few times in each direction. When you are satisfied with your performance, begin to increase the loop to somewhere between the quarter line and centerline, then on to a full loop to the centerline and back. At this point, you can be satisfied that your horse is strong and balanced enough for this exercise.

Once you have accomplished this, you can now direct your attention to yourself and your skill in giving the aids. Once again, ride a loop from the rail to the quarter line and back, but this time begin to lessen the loop, making it more and more shallow. Instead of asking more strength and balance from your horse, the exercise is now asking you to focus on your ability to position your horse subtly and accurately. Your goal is to be able to ride a loop that comes only one or two meters off the rail; but you must be very aware of the way you ask for the very slight change of bend, and of your horse's response to these subtle aids. Once you have mastered this, you can go back to riding the full rail-to-centerline loop, armed with a new skill and awareness.

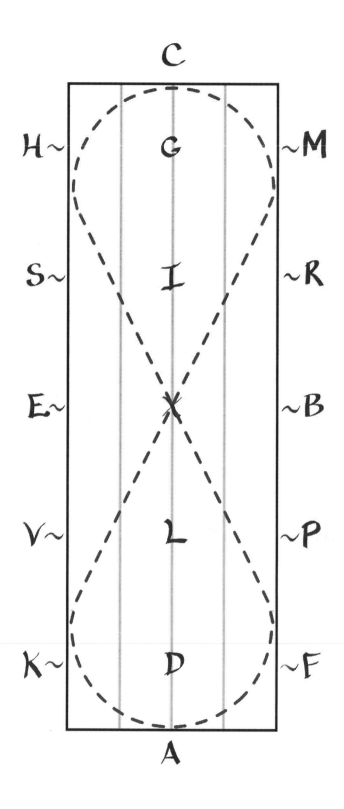

The Infinity

This exercise focuses on keeping a steady rhythm.

Ride a half circle, beginning four meters before F, touching the rail at A, and finishing back at the rail four meters after K. At this point head across the diagonal to four meters before M to then make another half circle, touching the rail at C and again four meters after H. Now head back across the diagonal to four meters before F and continue.

Concentrate on properly navigating your horse into a perfect half circle and on straight lines through X across the diagonal by using your corridor walls and force fields, and by drawing your lines ahead of you and using your video playback. As it takes more energy for the horse to make a turn or a circle, remember to ask a little more of him so he maintains a constant rhythm, and be prepared to check him so that he does not shoot out when you lead him onto the diagonal.

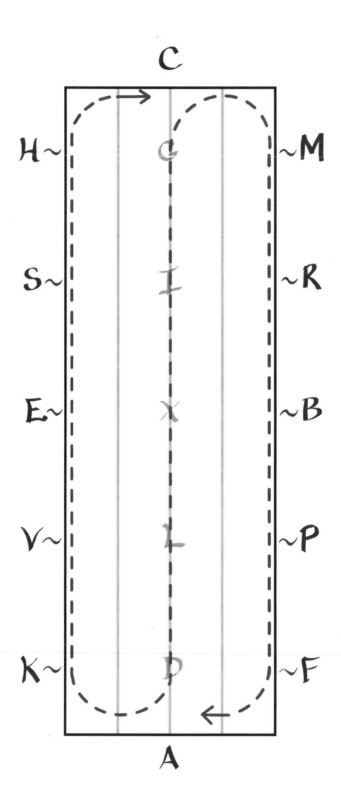

The Links

This exercise asks a little more from the horse in the turn and incorporates the use of the centerline in your sessions, which will be valuable when you begin to ride complete tests.

Ride down the long side, but at F make a ten-meter half circle to turn onto the centerline. As you approach F, draw a ten-meter half circle from the centerline back toward F and along the rail to your position. Give your horse a half-halt, allow him to feel your left corridor wall, and let the open swing of your inside hip lead him into this arc. As you finish your half circle and prepare to ride down the centerline, allow your horse to feel your right corridor wall to stop his turn and gently nudge him to encourage him to continue down the centerline on his own. When you reach C, change direction and head down the long side, beginning at H. Again, as you approach C, draw your line and prepare your horse for the half circle. At K again make a ten-meter half circle to turn down the centerline. When you reach C this time, track right to turn down the long side, beginning at M, and so on. Once you are comfortable with this exercise, you can begin to shorten the long side so that you ride a smaller and smaller oval, ending with a ten-meter circle.

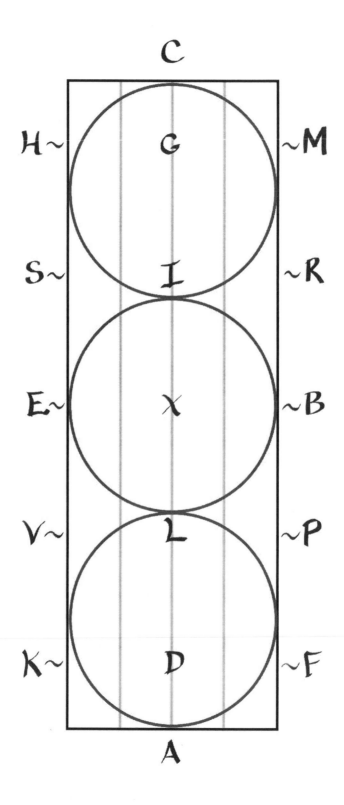

The Twenty-Meter Circle at Trot and Canter

Start practicing your circle at A or C so that you have the rails on three sides of it. Before you begin, mark in your mind the four points where the circle will touch the arena rail or the centerline. If possible, you can even mark the points on the rail with a bit of tape. For example, if you are at the A side of the arena, measure four meters down from both F and K; at the C end of the arena, measure four meters down from M and H. A third point will be the letter A or C. This will leave only one point on the circle, where it intersects the centerline two meters toward the center from the S–R or the V–P line, that you will have to eye on your own.

To ride an accurate circle, keep two things in mind: first, you must keep your horse aligned with the curved line of the circle but bent no more than that curve; and second, you must touch the four points of the circle for only one stride.

Thinking of the circle as a succession of short arcs, from F to A or A to K, for example, will help. If you are riding on the right rein, for example, and starting at A, draw your line from your point after K back to A and guide your horse along this line. While he is doing this, look over to your point on the centerline and draw another line back to your point after K. While you direct your horse onto this line, look over to your next arc at the point just after F and draw your line back to the centerline. Finally, draw your final arc from A back to the point just after F.

Use your corridor walls and force fields to guide your horse along the circle; your reins function only to keep his shoulders from bulging out.

Once you feel comfortable with this exercise, move the circle out into the arena so that the center is at X. Now you will only have two points on the rail (the letters E and B) to help you determine the circle, so you will need to learn to judge where to hit the centerline, two meters from I and L. This new circle will also prepare you for the next exercise, the figure eight, ridden in a standard arena.

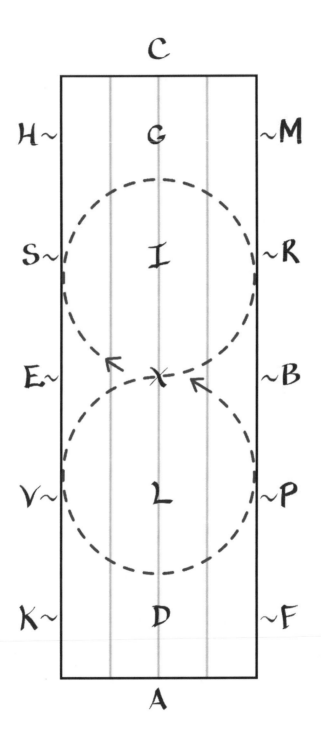

The Figure Eight

Once you have established a circle, you are now ready to begin the figure eight exercise at trot. The figure eight is simply two circles connected at one of their four points. Each time you cross this point, you change rein and change circle. If the change in circle comes too soon for you and your horse at first, simply trot twice around one circle, change to the second circle, trot that one twice, change again, and so on. Think of this as circles side by side.

Now, on top of keeping the horse properly positioned on the perfect circle, you will need to deal with a change in balance and direction where the two circles connect. In a standard arena, this shared point will be on the centerline two meters toward X from L, if you are starting at A, and two meters toward X from I, if you start at C. At this shared point, allow yourself to envision a short line perpendicular to the centerline where you can ride straight a few steps to give you time to prepare yourself and your horse for the change in direction. Make this change one step at a time. First, as you leave the rail heading for the centerline, change your posting diagonal to give your horse a heads-up that he will be changing direction. Then, as you ride across the centerline, you can concentrate on gradually shifting your horse's balance by allowing your horse to feel your inside corridor wall (the one that guards the center of the new circle you are about to travel on), which will then guide the horse into a new bend onto the new circle. Once you have changed your posting diagonal, given your horse your leg aids, and begun directing him onto the new circle, he should himself reposition his poll. Don't use your rein aids to pull him onto the new circle.

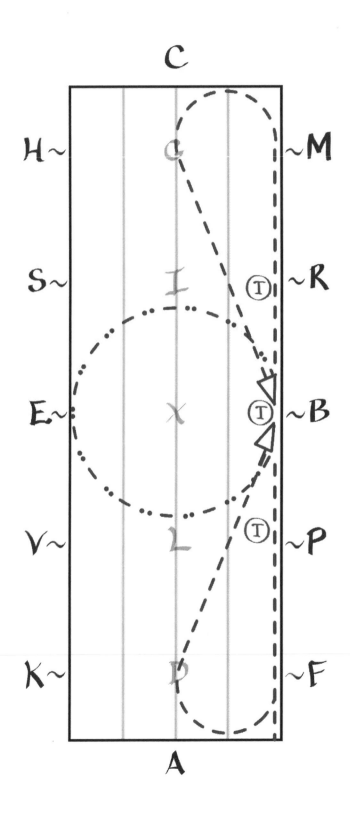

The Bow Tie

The bow tie combines two gaits and two figures. Start by riding a twenty-meter canter circle centered on X on the right rein. Remember to guide your horse with your corridor walls, and have your force fields at the ready. Keep your eyes up, drawing your half-arc lines back to you as you make your way around the circle. You will continue down the long side when you reach the rail at B, so as you approach B, half-halt your horse and allow him to feel your inside (right) corridor wall while you look down the rail. Now prepare for a transition to trot between B and F (in a standard-size arena, aim to come to a trot at P). Remember to regulate your canter, ask for your down transition, release, and keep your front open and strong. As you transition to the trot, look down to the centerline in front of A and draw a ten-meter half circle to F and back to where you are. At the end of the long side, half-halt your horse to help him hold his balance and keep his tempo, then make a ten-meter half circle onto the centerline. You will just touch the centerline and then continue diagonally back toward B. As you navigate your half circle, look toward B and draw your diagonal line back to the centerline. Allow your horse to feel your left corridor wall to complete the half circle and direct him toward B. Just before B, half-halt your horse and mentally prepare yourself for the left-lead canter depart at B. At B, pick up the left-lead canter to ride the twenty-meter circle around X. Keep your eyes up, draw your arc lines, use your video playback, guide with your corridor walls, and have your force fields at the ready. When you have reached B again, transition down to the trot and head down the long side toward M, and prepare for your transition to trot between B and M (in a standard-size arena, aim to come down at R). Regulate your canter, ask for your down transition, release, and keep your front open and strong. As you transition to the trot, look down to the centerline in front of C, draw a ten-meter half circle line back to M, and extend it back to your position. At the end of the long side, half-halt your horse, regulate your trot, prepare him to hold his balance and keep his tempo, make a ten-meter half circle, just touching the centerline, and continue diagonally back toward B. As you are navigating your half circle, look toward B and draw your diagonal line back to the centerline. Repeat the pattern a number of times.

Concentrate on the rhythm and relaxation of your horse throughout all of these changes in direction and gait; do not let him slow to a crawl in the ten-meter half circle, or rush into the twenty-meter canter circle. Try to be precise in placing your transitions.

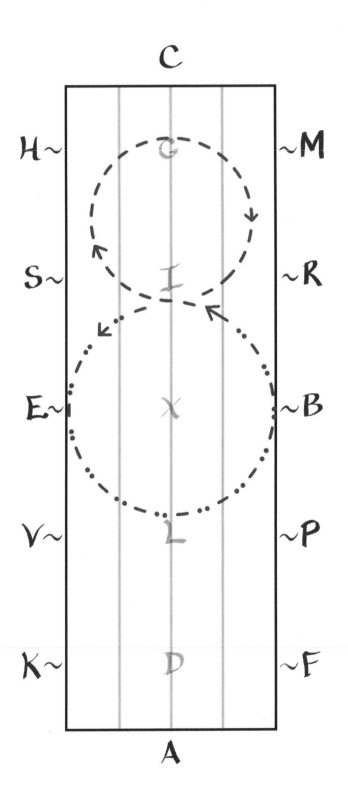

The Snowman

This exercise again combines trot and canter, but is a little more demanding than the bow tie. Where the figure eight uses two twenty-meter circles, this exercise uses a twenty-meter and a fifteen-meter circle connected where they touch the centerline. In a standard-size arena, this shared point will be on the centerline two meters toward X from L or I, depending on whether the large circle is at A or C.

Ride a twenty-meter circle at the canter. Keep your shoulder blades together, open your chest, look up, and draw your four arc lines to guide you. Let your hips swing as if you were skipping. Just before the shared point of both circles, half-halt your horse and allow him to feel your inside corridor wall to alert him to both the transition and change in bend and direction. Through the shared point, transition downward to the trot, change rein, and ride a fifteen-meter trot circle. Remember to release your down transition aid so that the horse can come properly into the trot, and to keep your front open and strong so that you do not pitch forward. While you are transitioning, look up and begin drawing your smaller arc lines to guide you through the fifteen-meter trot circle. As you approach the shared point again, mentally prepare yourself to ask for the canter depart and change of direction and bend. Half-halt your horse; then, as you again reach the shared point, change rein, ask for a canter, and ride the twenty-meter circle again. Ride this a few times in one direction and then in the other.

Not only does this exercise ask for increased ability to navigate, hold your balance, and remain on the circle, but it is also especially good for horses that have difficulty picking up the correct lead.

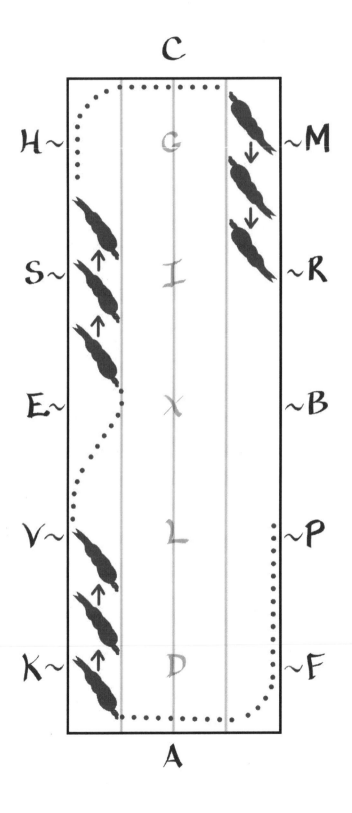

The Head-To-The-Wall Leg Yield

Many trainers use the head-to-the-wall leg yield to begin the lateral movements, as the rail serves as a natural check to the horse's forward movement. Typically, after a ten-meter circle in the corner, the horse is asked to change bend so that he faces out of the arena as he progresses down the long side. The version here, created by Major Anders Lindgren, drops the ten-meter circle and breaks up the head-to-the-wall leg yield into two sets for each long side.

To ask for the leg yield, weight the inside seat bone slightly, but be careful to keep your outside leg long. Ideally, you can ride the leg yield with both legs at the girth, but sliding either leg back will bring more influence to that side of the haunch. In other words, if your horse's haunches are trailing and you are keeping him straight and correct with your rein aids, you may want to bring the inside leg just behind the girth to push the horse forward and sideways. If your horse's haunches begin to lead, just slide the outside leg back a little to bring them back into correct position. Use the inside rein to create a little flexion at the poll only; be careful not to overbend the horse's neck and cause him to jackknife. You may give a little with the outside rein to help with flexion, but watch that the outside shoulder does not pop out.

On the right rein, ride from P to A. At A, you will ride a short diagonal to K. As you approach A, look over to K, draw your diagonal line back to A, and half-halt your horse to alert him that something is going to happen. At K you will ride a head-to-the-wall leg yield to V, so as you approach K, mentally prepare yourself to lead your horse into the leg yield as you look down toward V. As you approach V, look to the quarter line up by E and draw your half-loop line back to V while you half-halt your horse to prepare him. At V straighten the horse and ride a small loop to the quarter line at the BXE axis, and as you ride this draw your second half of the loop from S back to the quarter line as you prepare your horse for the change in bend. Then lead the horse back to the rail at S. As you approach S, mentally prepare yourself to give the leg-yield aids. When you reach the rail, continue down the long side in the head-to-the-wall leg yield to H and then straighten the horse again. Repeat this process along the opposite long side, starting with a short diagonal from C to M.

Start the exercise in the walk, and later progress to the trot. When you and the horse have the idea of leg yield down, you might progress to yielding along a diagonal to or away from the rail, keeping the horse's body parallel to the rail, as in the first-level tests.

Part 4

A Lunging Primer

In this little primer, I hope to introduce the horse enthusiast to two basic aspects of lunging. First, I define lunging as the act of properly seeing the horse. Second, instead of getting bogged down in tack fetishism, I will attempt to address what actually goes on during a lunging session, and set forth the techniques and strategies of lunging.

The fundamental basis of riding is feel. This feel is not mystical or mysterious, but comes from an understanding of the biomechanics of the horse and rider, an ability to concentrate, a measure of discipline, and some modicum of talent. The medium of lunging, however, is sight. Whereas a blind person could conceivably ride a horse quite well, it is unlikely that he could lunge one. In lunging we bend our concentration, discipline, and understanding of the biomechanics of the horse to what our eye tells us. And because this primer concerns itself with training our eye, it can be of interest even to those who do not lunge.

A great aspect of lunging a horse is the simple enjoyment of watching him work. Rare are the occasions on which we see our horse "performing," as it were, since watching him at liberty in the pasture is not the same as seeing him applying himself to his job. Watching him move well on the lunge allows us to get excited about our horse and instills in us a desire to rise to meet his ability when we ride him.

Seeing a horse move with our own eyes can also help us better understand what we are feeling when riding him. Just as that wonderful feeling of balance and movement while on the horse lies behind our desire to become better riders and improve our horse's movement, seeing the horse move on the lunge sharpens our eye and creates in us a desire to better him in his lunge work. As we learn to become attentive to the feel of the horse under us, to feel his impulsion, his stiffness, his throughness, his sluggishness, we learn to guide, correct, and praise him. Lunging requires of us a sharp eye so that we can see exactly what lies behind our horse's strengths and weaknesses.

The first section of this primer will discuss what we see when we watch a horse move. The remaining sections concern themselves with the setting, the tools, and the strategies of lunging. In "The Power of Pi," I stress the importance of setting up the twenty-meter circle. In "The Tools of Lunging," I explain the use of the voice, whip, lunge, and body commands. And finally, in "Putting It All Together," we discuss strategies for establishing lunging basics.

Viewing the Horse in Movement

> *What does a horse look like when he is moving correctly, when he is*
>   *moving with grace and beauty?*
> *What are the underlying biomechanics of this graceful beauty?*

These two questions constitute the fundamental basis of all lunge work. It is helpful to frame these questions with a comparison to sculpting. When a sculptor begins chipping away at his marble, he has an image in his mind of what he is sculpting. This image gives him his goal. But the marble itself also informs and guides each movement of his chisel, as if the sculpture that is in the process of coming into existence comes to meet the sculptor who is in the process of attempting to realize his ideal.

With lunging, we too have an image, a goal, of the horse moving correctly with power, grace, and beauty, but this image is a general paradigm. When we begin to work with a horse, he also brings his own conformation, desire, and ability to the work. Just as the sculpture is becoming itself as the sculptor is fashioning his ideal, so it is that our work with horses comes from a combination of our general knowledge and aesthetics of horses and the singular abilities of each horse. It is not enough for us to see rhythm or relaxation; we must learn to see the right rhythm for each individual horse, or what relaxation looks like for each individual horse.

Furthermore, it is one thing to see this in a horse, and another thing to understand it—just as it is one thing to recognize a nice mover out at a show or on a DVD, but quite another thing to be able to put your finger on just what makes this horse stand out. A number of clues do exist that can help us recognize good movement, however; use these to formulate an idea of how your horse is moving and what might improve him.

Overstriding. As explained in part 1 of this volume, "General Principles," when the horse's back is relaxed and his stomach muscles are engaged, his croup will drop, his back will lift, and his hind legs will be able to reach farther under him. When the horse is walking on the lunge, note where he places his hind feet in relation to his fronts. Does his hind foot step into the hoofprint left by his front foot? This is called tracking up. Or does his hind foot step beyond the hoofprint of his front foot and make a new print? When he does the latter, we call it overstriding. A horse's conformation—a very short back, long legs, or sickle hocks, for example—can make it possible for him to overstride even in the absence of relaxation and without the circle of muscles working properly, so be careful to factor this into your evaluation.

The neck muscles. Do not be overly concerned about the position of the horse's head. Look instead at his neck. If the horse is coming through from behind and over his topline, the muscles in front of his wither and over the top of his neck will pulse. If his neck is working properly, his head will follow. Just as it is detrimental to pull the horse's head onto the vertical with your hands while riding, so it is to constrain him too tightly with side reins. All too often riders' concern with the position of the horse's head comes from a lack of understanding of the horse as a whole; they have only learned that the horse should have his head on the vertical and so place it there by force without understanding that the horse's head will come to rest on the vertical, or slightly in front of it, when his entire body is traveling naturally. At the walk, the horse stretches his neck out with each stride, and for this reason it is advisable to ride the walk on lower-level horses with a long rein. For this reason also one should never use side reins on a horse at the walk. At the trot, the neck will hold its position, but you will still see the top muscles flexing when the horse is working through. If the horse is not working properly, you may see the underside of his neck bulging, or a cramped tightness (often betrayed by wrinkles in the skin) in front of his withers. The responsible lunger or rider will always encourage the horse's neck to stretch out; as the horse builds muscle on the top of his neck through natural and beautiful movement, the neck will develop an arch honestly.

The double triangle. Notice, as the horse travels around you on the lunge, that the two front legs and the two back legs each form a triangle that opens and closes. When the horse moves properly, these two triangles should open to the same width. When the triangle that the two hind legs create is much smaller than that of the front legs, for example, it is a sign that he is on the forehand, and that his hind legs are stiff, most likely because his back is tight. As his back loosens and his balance shifts, you should see a change in this triangle.

The ears and tail. A relaxed and attentive horse will have his ears out to the side and his tail relaxed and swaying in the rhythm of his stride. If agitated, the horse will swish his tail violently. If he is nervous or inattentive, his ears will flick this way and that, or prick forward tensely.

The slinky cat. As the horse relaxes into his rhythm, as his back lifts, as his hind legs come up to step beyond his front hoofprints, as the double triangles come to match, as his ears turn out to the side and his tail sways softly, the horse starts to take on a slinky, loose feeling. Train your eyes to zero in on the various details of a horse's body as he moves, but then zoom out and take in the whole picture. Don't get caught up in just looking at the overstride, for example. No one small detail gives the whole picture. Continually changing your focus from a detail to the whole horse will give you the information that you need to adjust your lunge work.

Balance. When the horse is traveling correctly, he will give the impression of being higher and lighter in front. If he is not working from behind and his hind legs do not come up underneath him and create a thrust forward, the horse can give the impression of having his hind end filled with helium, as if it is floating up off the ground a little as the horse travels, much like a person walking on his hands. Train your eye to decipher the difference between the horse stretching his head down, and therefore lifting his back, as he pushes off properly from behind, and the horse that is traveling on the forehand. Again, the head position will not help us; instead, it is the overall balance of his body, the position of his withers compared to his hind end, and the looseness of his shoulders that clue us in to whether he is on the forehand or not.

Cadence. In romantic movies, lovers run from a distance into each other's arms in slow motion. Something of this romance enters into the horse when, as he is going along, moving nicely from behind, and has taken on that slinky-cat look, all of a sudden everything seems to enter into slightly slower motion. He is still trotting around on the lunge at the same tempo, but somehow the lift in his body, the air in his stride, the upward movement that is the result of self-carriage, collection, and of taking a little more weight onto his hind end, clicks in. The quality of time seems to have been altered.

The Power of Pi

The circle is the glue of lunging. When we first begin a relationship with a horse, we must declare ourselves the leader, or herd sire. Once we have earned the horse's respect, we must then convince him that we are worthy of being followed. In lunging, this translates into first getting the horse's attention. While bringing him out to the arena, you must begin to talk to him and to lead him in such a way that he turns his mind to you and the job at hand. This does not always mean that he will follow your lead or give you what you ask for, but the dialogue has started. Work for a time when, as you walk out to the arena, you are looking ahead at other things and he is keeping his attention on you, instead of you constantly attending to him as he looks out for something to spook at or eat.

Once you have the horse's attention, you must start to convince him to follow you by first giving him a simple and understandable job. In the arena, traveling on the circle is this first job. Once the horse has been convinced to travel on the circle, he can then be asked to keep a steady tempo. By clearing all questions and worries from his mind and by giving him to understand that he need only travel the circle at an even tempo, the lunger allows him to settle into a relaxed state. Once you have established the circle, you have established a calm in the horse and a readiness to follow your lead.

Because a smaller circle puts more stress on the horse's joints and demands more work from his muscles, keeping the horse out on a large twenty-meter circle will help establish rhythm and relaxation. Sometimes it can be hard to maintain control of the horse when he is that far away.

A horse just learning his circle, or a spoiled horse that is acting up, for example, can be the source of much frustration for the lunger.

There are three main strategies for first establishing a good twenty-meter circle. The first is the classical method, which uses two people. The trainer stands in the middle and holds the lunge line and whip, while an assistant walks beside the horse on the inside. Once the walk and halt commands are established in this way, the assistant then moves to the outside of the horse to allow the relationship between the trainer and the horse to strengthen. Finally, the assistant simply walks away from the horse and allows him to continue on his own. Though it's a proven way of starting a horse on the lunge, this method is unfortunately not very practical for the average horse owner today.

The second method is to lead the horse out onto the twenty-meter circle yourself and to gradually move toward the center while leaving the horse out on the circle. This keeps the horse out on the large circle, but allows the lunger to adjust the length of the lunge line and therefore her control.

The third method is to first establish a smaller circle, perhaps ten meters across. When the horse settles into this circle, the lunger can then ask him to go out until he reaches the twenty-meter circle. If the lunger begins to lose control, she can simply begin to bring the horse back to the smaller circle. This makes use of one of the golden rules of training a horse: give the horse a choice of two options. In this case, he can travel the smaller, more difficult circle, or if he settles, he can go out to the easier-to-travel larger circle.

Whatever method you use, your objective when lunging the horse at this level is to get him relaxed and moving at an even rhythm on the twenty-meter circle.

The Tools of Lunging

The lunger has five main tools at her disposal to create a productive lunge session: her voice, the lunge whip, the lunge line, her own body movement, and side reins.

The voice

It cannot be stressed enough just how important voice commands are while lunging. All lunging relies on an intense communication between lunger and horse, so the clearer and more meaningful your voice commands are, the better. Remember also that the horse does not speak our language, but listens instead to the tone and cadence of our speech. Be sure to remain consistent in all of your voice commands.

The basic voice commands are "Walk," "Trot," "Canter," and "Whoa" or "Ho." Be sure to pronounce these words in such a way as to clearly distinguish them in the horse's mind. It is also useful to modify these voice commands into up-transition and down-transition versions. Thus the voice command "Walk" can be used to ask for an up transition from halt or a down transition from trot, for example, and must be spoken differently in each case.

To distinguish the up-transition "Walk" from the down-transition command, the lunger might instill a sense of energy to the command and even add a word: "WALK on!" Draw this command out a little to hold the "w" so that you add lift to the phrase, "WWWALK on!" To create a down-transition command to walk, draw out the "a" and deflate the energy from the word: "Waaaaaaaalk."

Similarly, the "Trot" command can be modified as be an up- or down-transition command by drawing it out into two syllables for the up transition—"TEEEE-rot!"—and by drawing out the vowel for a down transition—"Traaaaaaaaaaat."

"Canter" and "Ho" are always up- and down-transition commands respectively, so that "Canter" should always be spoken with energy—"CAN-ter!"—and "Ho" always deflated—"Whooooaaa."

Laid out on paper like this, these commands and their intonations seem obvious, but I can assure you that many forget this basic rule of speaking to the horse when also concentrating on everything else they need to be watching for and doing while lunging a horse.

In addition to these basic commands, there is another set, which we shall call the modifying commands. The ones I use are "and," "come," "ho ho," and "out." "And" is used to give the horse a heads-up, much like a half-halt, and is spoken with a drawn-out, lead-in feeling. When asking for the canter, for example, the lunger can say, "aaand CAN-ter!" "Come" is used to ask for more impulsion from a horse at any gait, and is spoken with urgency. "Ho ho" can be used to settle or quiet a horse, and is spoken with a soft two-note lilt: "ho hooa." Finally, "out" serves to send the horse back out onto the circle when he begins to fall in, and is spoken very matter-of-factly.

The most effective and important use of voice is in praising your horse. The ideal session has the horse willingly responding to praise from the lunger, not obeying in fear of retribution. "Good boy!" or "Good girl!" are easy and effective praises. Note that they can be spoken also with an energizing or calming voice. Thus if a horse is rushing you may say, "Ho hoooa, goood boy," to relax and calm him when he responds to the "ho ho" command, but if you are encouraging him to give you more trot, you would say, "Come! Come! Good BOY!"

Keep your voice commands positive so that your horse understands that he is doing a good thing when he responds to you. And finally, though voice commands are essential, overuse of the voice, just like overuse of any aid, can cause a horse to tune out. Use your words with care. Do not put yourself in the position of having to ask the horse eight or ten times to come from a trot to a walk.

The Lunge Whip

The lunge whip is similar to the rider's leg or seat in that it regulates the forwardness of the horse, and should be held so that it points to an area just behind the horse's haunches. The horse should not fear the lunge whip, but he should respond to it.

The basic concept behind the power of the lunge whip concerns its position in relation to the horse. If you hold the whip pointing back behind you so that the horse cannot see it, it has no power, no effect. As you move the whip, as in an arc, out from behind you, it gains in effectiveness. When it gets to where it is pointing just behind the horse's hindquarters, it has the most power as a driving force. As it travels up toward the horse's shoulder, its power gradually changes from a driving force to a pushing-out force. Finally, if the whip is pointed beyond the shoulder, to the horse's head or just in front of him, it then begins to act as an obstruction to the horse's concentration. All use of the whip, therefore, should keep this in mind. Below are six basic movements made with the whip, as examples of the varying ways in which it can be used to affect the horse: the metronome, the pop, the raise, the shoulder-point, and retiring the whip.

The metronome is the most common movement for lunging, and is performed by holding the whip pointed down toward the sand and calmly but continually moving the tip of the solid part of the lunge whip slightly left then slightly right in a back-and-forth manner. This sets the rhythm you wish the horse to travel in while acting as a constant reminder to the horse that he is being asked to move forward. Do not make this motion too active, or it may overstress the horse, but never leave your whip still. If your horse overreacts to this small movement, then you must spend time familiarizing him with the whip so that he no longer fears it. Spend a few sessions just allowing the horse to sniff the whip and, when he allows it, gently caressing his neck and flank with it. The importance of being able to keep the whip gently active is that it allows the lunger to make subtle changes in the action of the whip, and thus control the forward movement more precisely. If you hold the whip still and only use it to goad the horse forward when he begins to lag, you risk surprising or startling him into an overreaction. But if you keep the whip gently swaying back and forth like a metronome, you can adjust this aid quickly and with precision.

The raise is a way to ask for a little more impulsion from the horse. Most times a more energetic movement of the metronome is enough to bring a horse forward, but when this is not enough, you can move to the raise. Simply raising the tip of the lunge whip up to shoulder level (but still pointed just behind his haunch) should be enough. If needed, the lunger can keep the whip up at this level for a few strides to confirm the command.

The pop is a crack of the whip and is used to urge a stubborn or lazy horse forward. When neither the metronome or the raise give the desired effect, use the pop. The pop can also be used to create a quicker and more succinct response to an up-transition command. Always direct the pop of the whip just behind the horse.

The shoulder-point underlines the "Out" voice command. If the horse begins to fall in on the circle, point the tip of the lunge whip at his shoulder as you give the voice command. A variation of the shoulder-point is the fan. By moving, or fanning, the whip smoothly back and forth in front of you and between you and the flank of the horse, you will create a very physical barrier for a horse that tends to fall in on the circle.

The hide is used when calming a nervous horse. Point the whip behind you so that it is no longer visible to the horse. When he is again calm, bring the whip around little by little until it can again remain pointing just behind his haunches.

The retiring of the whip is used during tantrums or when a horse has been spooked. While trying to regain control and calm, the lunger can tuck the whip under her arm, with the point facing behind her, so that the whip becomes invisible to the horse, and so that she has two hands free to regain control.

Practice handling your lunge whip. You should be able to easily and quickly move it from pointing forward to pointing backward without startling the horse. Sometimes it might be necessary to hold the whip in the middle so that it does not jut out as far when introducing it to a nervous horse. Other times you may need to gather the loose end of the whip into your whip hand to lessen the pressure on a nervous horse without raising the whip in the air and startling him.

The Lunge Line
The lunge line acts much like the rider's reins and seat aids in that it regulates the impulsion that is coming through from behind and it steers the horse, describing the circle that the horse should follow.

Attach the lunge line to the middle ring on the cavesson. If you are not using a cavesson, there are two ways to connect the lunge line to the horse's bridle. The first is to thread the line through the inside bit ring, up over the horse's poll, down the outside of his head and attach it to the outside bit ring. This method puts pressure on the horse's poll, with the idea of preventing him from throwing his head up. Unfortunately, some horses, instead of yielding, will strain upward against this pressure. The second, preferable method is to thread the line through the inside bit ring, but this time allow it to go under the horse's chin and be attached to the outside bit ring. This method also aims for a more even contact on both sides of the horse's mouth, but avoids putting pressure on his poll.

When you have begun to master the art of lunging, you will develop an elastic contact through the lunge line that will allow you to apply rein aids much the same as those we use while riding: the yielding, the nonyielding, the regulating, and the supporting. Below, however, are four basic lunge line movements that you might want to consider at this point: the tug and release, the hand squeeze, the leading hand, and the upward pull.

The tug and release is used to check the horse's wayward movement. It can be used to keep the horse's head from facing out of the circle, and thus help both to establish attention and to create a proper bend, but it can also be used to check a rushing horse. As in riding, the release of the aid is the aid; it is very important to remember to release any built-up pressure on the lunge line. Perform the tug and release smoothly; do not jerk violently.

The hand squeeze is a more subtle version of the tug and release and is performed, as its name states, by squeezing and relaxing the hand. This should help check the horse's forward movement enough to help rebalance him by redistributing his weight to his haunches. It should match in its use the combination of unyielding/yielding rein aid that we use while riding.

The leading hand is used to keep a horse out on the circle. As the horse begins to fall in, lift your hand up to shoulder level and out a little from your side, as if leading the horse forward and away. Because he believes he must now move around this obstacle, the horse will begin to move straight, which will thus lead him back onto the circle. This aid should be performed in a smooth motion as if one were asking someone, "Step this way, please." Aside from the psychological obstacle that this hand gesture presents to the horse, it also creates a small physical straight line with the lunge line, so that if the horse keeps the contact on the line, he will have no other choice but to move out onto the circle.

The upward pull can be used to stop a horse from dropping his head at the walk or trot. It is also used at the canter to help lift the horse up in front. Simply raise your hand as he begins the upward moment of his canter stride. This lunge line movement is only effective if it is combined with the voice and whip aid, so as not to teach the horse to hang on your hand.

Remember that these basic lunge line movements should be performed with the same subtlety with which we hope to perform our rein aids while riding. Try to make them as invisible as possible.

The Body
The center point of the circle is the lunger's body. When the lunger holds her whip and line correctly, with her hands at her hips, the whip pointing to an area just behind the horse, the lunge line stretching out to its nose, and her body positioned at the horse's shoulder, she also creates a triangle with her body as one of its points. Think of this triangle as the triangle of power and of the lunger's point as the energizing force. The circle that you ask your horse to travel is the extent of your influence. Lunging then becomes the movement of this triangle of power within the circle of influence.

Aside from the voice, whip, and line, the lunger can also use her body to influence the horse. Three techniques for this are stepping out, moving quickly to the side, and the use of the "hip lock."

Stepping out refers to a quick and pronounced step toward the horse that is used either to encourage more forward movement or to help push him back onto the circle.

The quick movement to the side toward the direction of movement helps keep the horse from cutting in on the circle.

The hip lock is used when a horse becomes too strong. Bring your whip hand behind your buttock and use your leg and core muscles to hold yourself in balance while you establish control.

The Side Reins
There is really very little that can be accomplished on the lunge without side reins. Side reins support and encourage the horse to keep his frame; they should not be tightened to a point where they are forcing a horse into a shape. Their length should remain consistent with the horse's own

ability. If the horse travels on the lunge with an open mouth and straining on the bit, with his hind legs taking short steps, then the side reins are too short. If he travels with the reins sagging and bouncing under him, his frame flattened out, then they are so long as to be ineffective. These two examples represent the extremes; experience and a sharp eye will help you detect the more subtle effects of side reins.

Adjusting side reins will be an ongoing procedure when lunging. Some days you may find that you need to increase or shorten them due to your horse's attitude and energy on that day. During a lunge session you may also decide to adjust the side reins as a result of the horse warming to his work. And of course over a longer period of time, as your horse progresses in his training, adjusting his balance and frame accordingly, you will need to shorten the side reins now and again to reflect this change.

Attach the side reins to the large ring of the surcingle that rests on the horse's flank. If you are not using a surcingle, attach the side reins to the billet straps of your saddle so that the side reins are even with the horse's shoulder.

Putting It All Together

Lunging plays an important role in three main areas of training the horse. First, when the horse is young or green, it is beneficial to introduce him first on the lunge to the basics of his work. Here he will become familiar with the arena, the trainer, the tack, and the basic contract between horse and rider, as well as accustoming himself to the work week. Second, when a horse has been spoiled by improper training, lunging can be a powerful tool in reestablishing the relationship between horse and rider as a beginning to proper training. And third, lunging can increase the opportunity for the rider to ride in harmony on her horse, since after correct training on the lunge, the horse will be better able to help the rider find her own balance and confidence. Correct lunge training prepares the horse physically and mentally for a rider on his back, while also giving the future rider an appreciation of and joy in her horse's ability. This in turn creates an eagerness to ride correctly and with sensitivity to the horse. Simply put, there is a great moral-boosting joy in watching your horse move beautifully.

An important aside: Readers of this book—that is, those interested in preparing their horse for the basics of dressage training—will be taking up lunging from one of the three backgrounds just described. Though working with a qualified trainer is always recommended, it is especially so if you are trying to start a green horse.

All work with your horse consists of energizing his body while calming his mind, and lunging is no exception. The first aim of lunging, therefore, should be to establish the horse on the circle at an energetic and forward rhythm with a relaxed mind and supple muscles. The horse cannot simply travel at any consistent rhythm; he cannot be allowed to rush at too fast a speed nor drag himself around at a snail's pace. He must have a look of purpose, and his rhythm should be that of a horse who is using his muscles. Relaxation does not mean that his muscles should be limp. On the contrary, he should be asked to work, but in such a way that his mind is relaxed and receptive and his body is supple and elastic.

Getting a horse to move in rhythm and relaxation on the lunge should be the main objective for the reader of this primer. To bring a horse to this point requires a sharp eye and quick reactions from the lunger. She must be constantly regulating the progress of her horse, ready to step in when he loses impulsion or begins to rush, or when he deviates from his circle or begins to allow his attention to wander. Later, while still constantly monitoring these aspects of the horse's movement, she will be able to introduce exercises on the lunge that gradually adjust his balance, so that he begins his journey toward setting himself back on his haunches.

The Giraffe and the Elephant's Trunk: Introducing Contact

At training level, we are first interested in properly introducing the horse to the lunge and establishing the circle, so that he may be asked to work in rhythm and relaxation. Our first two concerns, then, will be to introduce the horse to bit contact and to establish a good circle. Introducing the horse to bit contact should not be confused with connection, the third step in the training pyramid. Introducing the horse to bit contact here simply means allowing him to be comfortable with a bit in his mouth.

To bring a horse to the arena for his first day of lunging and simply send him out on the end of the lunge line is almost guaranteed to result in trouble, and shows an ignorance of the very concept of lunging. No matter how trained you know your horse to be, and how confident you feel in your ability to lunge, always start your first session by simply walking side by side with the horse around the circle in both directions. You will notice that just walking on the off side of the horse, something we never do otherwise, will be strange for both of you. And it may be that all you do in your first session, or sessions even, is to simply walk the horse around the circle in order to lay the groundwork. But persevere, and you will be rewarded. Once your horse is comfortable with the circle at the walk, you can then introduce the trot. (For more on establishing the circle, review "The Power of Pi," above.)

Once you have the horse traveling at the walk and trot on the circle, it is time to introduce him to the side reins. Even if the horse has been ridden extensively, he may still not have the proper relationship with the bit for lunging and for true dressage work, so do not overlook the importance of proceeding responsibly when introducing the horse to side reins. Understanding the effect of the side reins on a horse comes from experience, as does knowing how and when to shorten them. Unfortunately, very little can be explained on paper about this, and to a great degree the lunger will be left to trial and error, if she does not have the benefit of working alongside a qualified trainer.

For this reason, work conservatively. Begin by attaching only the outside side rein, making it so long that it sags. When you feel that the horse is comfortable with this, attach the inside side rein. Do not forget that when you change direction, you will need to again introduce only the outside side rein, even if the horse was traveling well with both in the first direction. As with introducing the horse to the circle, familiarizing the horse with side reins must be done through a number of small steps. It may be that you can work quickly through these steps, maybe even several in one session, but these steps must never be skipped or disregarded. Remember also that the side reins should not truss the horse up into a frame. You will notice that even if the side reins seem loose, they will affect his carriage and movement. They serve as a reminder and as a suggestion to the horse to travel well; they do not force him to do so. A good rule of thumb to follow until you have developed a keener eye is to adjust the side reins a hole or two longer than how the horse carries himself, so that the side reins follow the horse's frame and are there when he becomes lazy or forgets himself. Just as in riding, we want the horse to use himself on his own and to make his own mistakes. Our job is to support and encourage him, not hold him up and push him.

When we attach the side reins to the bit, we establish a regular, un-yielding yet undemanding contact between the bit and the horse's mouth. If the horse is unused to this, he will go through a number of evasions before settling to the new relationship. Some horses will pull their head up, straining at the side reins and traveling much like a giraffe. Others will drop their heads down to the sand, wagging their neck and head like the trunk of an elephant. In focusing on the bit contact, the giraffe will be oblivious to how uncomfortable it is to travel in such a way, and the elephant's trunk, to how often it ends up kicking itself as it travels the circle.

Energizing the Horse: The Basis of Rhythm

When first starting a horse on the lunge, the lunger will more than likely be confronted with a horse that reacts to this new situation either by rushing or by balking, halting, or turning. Any reaction of this type on the part of the horse is an impediment to our first goal of establishing rhythm. The rushing horse increases his speed as he travels the circle; the balking horse will constantly interrupt the flow. Our first goal, then, is to establish rhythm.

If your horse begins to rush when you are only asking him to walk on the lunge, use either of the strategies discussed in "The Power of Pi," above. Either walk the twenty-meter circle with him or bring him into a small circle where you will be more effective in controlling him. If he is giving you too much trouble, you may need to go back a step to some leading basics. Lead him around the arena in various patterns, asking him to keep his shoulder even with yours while maintaining a respectful distance. Ask him to halt and walk on a number of times and in a number of different areas. When you are happy with his ability to listen, then you can return to the lunging circle.

However, just because your horse is attentive and obedient on the lunge at the walk, it does not mean that he will be so when you then ask him to trot. If you find that he begins to rush at the trot, you can employ one of two strategies. The first is to have patience and try to coax him down to a manageable trot through the use of your voice commands and the "hand squeeze" or "tug and release" aids with the lunge line. After the initial surprise of being asked to trot, and given gentle persistence in calming him, you may find that your horse will then begin to settle into work.

The other strategy that you may wish to apply is simply to let him trot only half a circle, and then ask him to come back to the walk. It is often effective to then halt the horse and pat him gently and reassuringly on the neck before sending him off into the trot again. Don't hesitate to use both strategies at the same time. Ask for the trot, then gently and patiently ask your horse to slow down a little. If he does slow a little, ask him to come down to the halt and pat and praise him before sending him off again. If he does not slow down, bring him down to the halt and calm and reassure him with your voice and a pat on the neck. Once he is traveling on a semblance of a circle at a more or less reasonable tempo, then it is time to concentrate on reassuring your horse that no more will be asked of him at this time. Through creating this safe zone, we give the horse the opportunity to relax into his work.

Calming the Mind: The Basis of Relaxation

Now that the horse is traveling a decent circle in a reasonably constant tempo, it is time to concentrate on relaxing him. There is a connection between rhythm and relaxation, since keeping him on a circle and going at a regular rhythm will generate relaxation, and encouraging relaxation will help keep the circle and the rhythm.

A way to approach this is to recognize that the beginning of rhythm is a physical matter; that is, it concerns the body of the horse. Relaxation adds a mental aspect. When encouraging relaxation in a horse, we are hoping to calm his mind, to assure him that all is well. But we are also, through calming his mind, asking him to relax his muscles so that he may move smoothly and with elasticity.

To relax a horse, we will use the same strategies that we used above to create rhythm, but the focus will be different. A horse that increases his speed as he travels the circle or constantly stops or balks requires a certain gentle firmness to help him concentrate on the circle. As long as you and the horse are engaged in a discussion on whether he will maintain the circle or not, you will not instill relaxation in the horse. The first step, then, will be to establish a fairly good circle; that is, the horse may still be nervous and swing out or in a little, but is generally describing some form of a circle. At this point, we must shift our focus to relaxing the horse by gradually enforcing a perfect circle while talking gently to him. Be careful not to overlunge the horse, but let him have enough time to adjust to the circle. Give him the down time to come to you. Don't bombard him with aids and talk. Let him figure it out a little, as long as you are there to maintain the circle and the rhythm. To do this, it is good to be familiar with a little mathematics.

Masters of the Circle—Eudoxus, Hui, Newton, and You

Eudoxus of Cnidus (410 or 408 BC – 355 or 347 BC), one of the greatest of classical Greek mathematicians, proved a number of mathematical statements about circles and their radii. The great Chinese mathematician, Liu Hui (429–400), was one of the greatest contributors to empirical solid geometry. And of course Sir Isaac Newton (1642–1727) shares with Gottfried Leibniz the credit for the development of the area of study known as calculus.

While we may not have time and space here to delve into the advancements these men have made in the minor sciences of geometry, astronomy, and the like, it is important to recognize what their endeavors have given to dressage. To master the basic lunging techniques, we may not need to go deeply into the principles of differential calculus, but we still need to grasp a few fundamentals of trajectories and arcs; we still need to understand just what is happening when a horse is moving around us in a perfect twenty-meter circle, and more importantly, what corrections must be applied when he is not.

Let us first establish two aspects of the movement of the horse. First, in order to describe a circle, the horse must travel along a series of four arcs. Second, the circle is also made up of an incalculable number of small straight lines. So, an understanding of arcs and trajectories is needed to properly lunge a horse.

Figure 10. Using the Lunge Line to Affect the Horse's Trajectory.

The establishment of the circle on the lunge is, as we have said, the glue of lunging. It is the construction of this circle that will give the horse his safe zone. The closer you bring your horse to a perfect circle, the more consistent his tempo will be. It's worth saying again: if you can make the horse travel on a perfect twenty-meter circle, you will also make his rhythm consistent. The very act of slowing, balking, rushing, spooking, shying, or any other movement that affects the horse's tempo will invariably take him off the circle, because these movements are physical representations of his wandering from the circle path in his mind. Creating a circle and establishing tempo are not the exact same thing, but they are two sides of the same coin.

To maintain the circle you will need to deal with an evasion at the momentit happens, and prepare for the eventual return of that evasion. If you are lunging a horse that suddenly begins to veer in on the circle, do not try to immediately send the horse back onto the circle. More than likely, this will cause him to move in the opposite direction, out of the circle, so that you will then feel the need to yank him back onto the circle, which in turn will only send him veering in on the circle again, and so on, so that he begins to travel a jagged line in and out of the circle as he goes around you. At this point you have utterly lost control of the situation. Instead, if he begins to veer in on the circle, for example, correct his trajectory slightly, so that he will gradually return to the circle without disrupting his rhythm or bend.

There are two tools we have to correct the horse's trajectory: the lunge line and the lunge whip.

If we think of the lunge line as the radius of the circle, with our hand as the center point, we can shift our circle, and thereby create a new trajectory, simply by moving our hand. Be aware that it takes only a slight change in the center of a circle to create a rather large change out at the perimeter of that circle. Simply moving our hand over a foot will make a large shift in the circle out at the horse.

In our math books the radius of a circle is constant. But in lunging, our radius is constant only as long as the horse accepts and keeps the contact with the bit. When a horse begins to fall into the circle, he is shortening the radius and therby creating a new circle. In order to ensure that our horse does not play with our radius, we must always keep him on the lunge line and maintaining contact with the bit.

Since he is maintaining contact with the bit, and because a circle is only a series of small straight lines, by encouraging him forward a little more with the lunge whip, that is, by encouraging him straight, we can adjust his trajectory to maintain our radius, and even shift our circle if need be.

It is a truism in lunging that if a horse goes wide or cuts in on a circle at a certain point, he will do so again at that same spot the next time around. Perhaps the magnetic quality of the barn draws him out of the circle on one side; perhaps he shies from a chair near the arena; perhaps he is startled by his shadow, and so on. Thus, when the horse strays from the circle, we can use our understanding of the circle as a series of arcs to place or fix the area where the horse went off course. In your mind, mark that spot as the center of one of the four arcs in the circle, so that the next time around you will be prepared to make the necessary correction.

The reason we think of the spot as the center of an arc is because we know that we will need to use our understanding of trajectories to correct the horse. In other words, we will need to begin correcting the horse before he reaches that same spot, so that he is already in an altered trajectory when he reaches it. This is why we prepare for the next time around on the circle instead of trying to do something at that moment. We cannot fall into the trap of the moment, but must instead think of the entire lunging session as a whole. We cannot fix the shy, the cutting in on the circle, or the blowing out of it once it has happened, for at that moment we have already lost control. What remains, then, is to learn from the incident and to begin again to actively lead the horse around the circle,

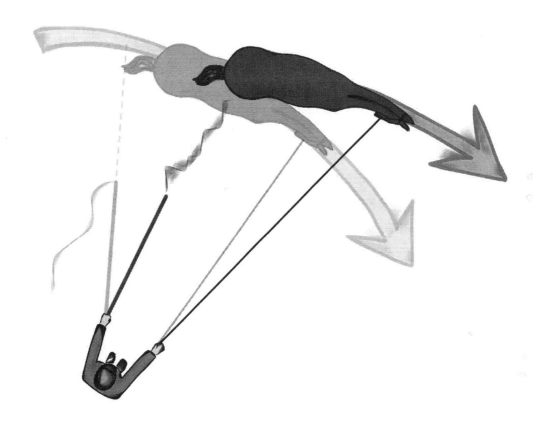

Figure 11. Using the Lunge Whip to Affect the Horse's Trajectory

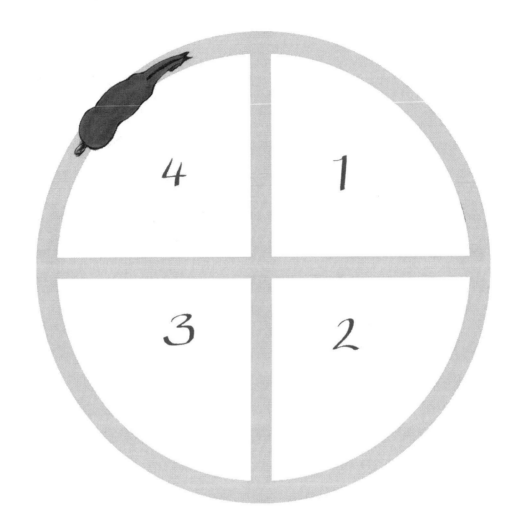

Figure 12. The Lunge Circle as Four Arcs

thereby reestablishing our relationship with the horse: Be with me, I will let nothing harm you. Trust me, I will take care of you.

So how do we correct the horse, you ask, before he reaches the troubled spot again? Let's say that the circle is divided into four arcs that are numbered in your mind as 1, 2, 3, and 4 (fig. 12). Now, while traveling somewhere in arc 3, your horse goes wide of the circle. The first step in correcting the horse will be in modifying the placement of these arcs in your mind so that the spot where the horse went wide is now at the center of arc 3. Meanwhile the horse travels through arcs 4 and 1. When he reaches arc 2, you will begin to calculate just how much of a correction you will need to make to have the horse on another trajectory when he enters arc 3. As he is passing into arc 3, then, you have already asked him to come in on the circle just enough to counteract his tendency to move out of it. Your combined tendencies will thus create an arc that reestablishes the perfect twenty-meter circle. If, instead, he cuts in on the circle at this point, you would be asking him to go out on the circle as he was passing into arc 3 to maintain the equilibrium. In short, the correction must be made before the trouble spot if the new trajectory is to take shape, and the correction is to work.

The Symmetry of the Oval

Let us leave the hard world of mathematics for one of flow, fluidity, and balance. While we are riding a horse, the subtlety of our aids is in direct relation to the quickness of our ability to react to the horse's movement. If we wait for the horse to completely give up any power in his hind legs, drop his back, and poke his head up like a giraffe, we have a lot of very obvious, and unseemly, corrections to make. However, if we can feel the loss of impulsion at its slightest hint, we can make a subtle half-halt or driving correction, one that will be invisible to the onlooker. And so it is with lunging.

If we wait for the horse to fly far away from the circle and then try to yank him back onto it, we will find ourselves with a horse cutting deeply into the circle he was leaving only a moment ago. Our unfortunate correction at this point will now have the horse on a trajectory flying out of the circle again, so that he will soon be describing an oval instead of a circle. In more extreme cases, the oval will be so exaggerated as to resemble a hot dog, before all chaos breaks out. Remember, the height of the wave that rises, is the depth of the trough that follows. For it is that quality of water, one that demands that we calm waves little by little in order to reach stillness, that should be in our mind while lunging. If there is a lot of movement in your bathwater, you will not be able to make it still by slapping the waves down at once. You must soften a little at a time.

So when your horse flies out of the circle, for example, remember first that it is not what you do at that precise moment that will help, so much as how you approach the entire circle. Because you are working with trajectories, once the horse has gone out of the circle, any attempt to pull him back into the circle will only affect the next arc, sending him cutting in on the circle. Instead, you must make a minimum of correction to stop him from continuing out of the circle and pulling the line out of your hand, while concentrating more on how he will be traveling in the next arc. Don't sacrifice the entire circle when one arc is compromised. Stop the horse from leaving you completely, and then immediately concentrate on adjusting his trajectory so that he returns smoothly onto the circle, while preparing in your mind where you will be making the correction in the near future to stop him from flying out of the circle again.

Obviously, the same approach applies when the horse cuts in on the circle. Stop him from running over you, and then find the smoothest trajectory that sends him back onto the circle, while preparing in your mind for when you will begin to push him out to counteract his desire to cut in.

In passing, there is another kind of oval—let us call it the barn oval—that can arise during lunging, whereby the same thing that attracts the horse out of the circle on one side will cause it to cut into the circle on the side directly opposite it. This situation is not one that comes from improper corrections, such as discussed above, but should be dealt with simply as two trouble spots in the circle.

Overcoming the Trouble Spot

Up to this point, we have discussed difficulties in maintaining the circle only in terms of a horse moving out of or in on the circle and how the use of trajectories can be employed to correct these situations. There are, of course, other disruptions that occur that cannot be overcome simply by a change in trajectory.

If, for example, there is a chair by the arena that the horse fears and shies from every time he passes it, no amount of trajectory tweaking is going to matter much in helping the horse to get over his fear; or more likely his evasion, for it is common for a horse who wishes to shirk his responsibilities to create a fear of some nearby object in hopes of getting out of work. At any rate, in these instances there are two corrections that can be made. Again, these corrections must also be made before the trouble spot.

First, sometimes a simple encouragement with the lunge whip will send a balking horse through a trouble spot. As he is about to enter the arc where the trouble spot lies, begin to encourage him forward or even request a change in gait from walk to trot, or trot to canter, to counteract the balkiness that you know he will soon show. If, on the other hand, he responds to this scary spot by speeding up, simply begin to set him back as he is about to enter the troubled arc so that you are already asking him to slow down even before he comes to the point where he wants to speed up. A stronger correction would simply be to ask him to come to the walk from the trot or trot from the canter at the beginning of this troubled arc. Be open to following an encouraging correction with a calming correction back to back, or in a number of successions, until you reach the smooth balance that is the steady tempo. Finally, once the horse has traveled the circle a couple of times while you make these corrections, allow the horse to face this trouble spot without any correction on your part. If you continue to make the corrections when they are not needed, you only play into the horse's idea that something is really there that requires special attention.

The other approach to a trouble spot is to demand that the horse pay more attention to you or your lunge line or whip. For example, as the horse enters the arc where he is prone to shying into the circle, raise the lunge whip and point it at his shoulder so that at that moment his attention is drawn toward this force that is coming from the middle of the circle and pushing him out. Transitions fall into this approach as well as the one above because they too require more concentration from the horse. You could also ask the horse to spiral in on the circle slightly and then spiral him out so that he enters the problem arc with the force of his motion going outward. Again, once you have made a correction a couple of times, let the horse travel the arc without a correction to allow him to do the right thing on his own.

Conclusion

This primer views the basics of lunging in much the same way that the handbook itself approaches the basics of dressage riding. To the uninformed, lunging a horse around a twenty-meter circle may seem too simplistic to warrant much serious analysis or concern. After reading these pages, the reader should now appreciate the skill required for a good basic lunge session, and be eager to accept the challenge of including it in her and her horse's education.

At this level, remember that your goal in the lunge session is to establish the first two steps of the training pyramid, rhythm and relaxation. Use the guidelines in this primer to develop your voice, whip, lunge, and body commands. Become adept at establishing a circle and use your understanding of trajectories to make your corrections. At this point concentrate mostly on keeping the circle. As your ability in this regard improves, begin using transitions to strengthen and rebalance your horse. My first level handbook, a sequel to this primer, delves deeper into seeing and affecting balance in your horse, and discusses a number of more advanced lunge exercises. For the time being, concentrate more on appreciating what you are looking at while watching the horse move in front of you. Zoom in to specific functions of his body, and then zoom out to the overall picture, and be attentive to the feeling you receive from that picture. And most of all, enjoy the beauty of your horse in motion.

Part 5

The Tests

Here we will first go through the definitions and explanations for each of the movements found in the training level tests and then walk through each of the tests in turn.

At training level you will either be riding in a standard arena, which measures twenty by sixty meters, or a small arena, which measures forty by twenty meters. The size of arena you ride in will affect the time you have to prepare for each movement. Straight lines, both along the rail and across the diagonal, will be shorter in the small arena, and the trot loop in test 3 will be shorter and steeper. Your visual cues for placing the twenty-meter circles will be different, as well. Figure 13 shows the placement of the twenty-meter circles that occur in the training level tests in a small and a standard arena.

The Individual Movements

The Medium Walk
The medium walk is a gait with four distinct beats: left hind, left fore, right

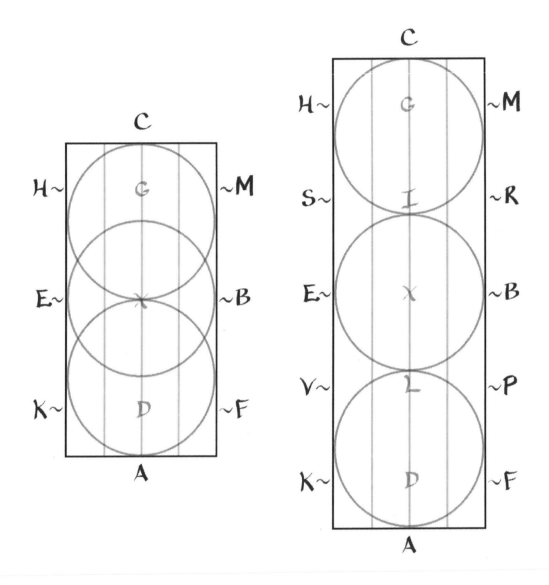

Figure 13. Arena Sizes

hind, right fore; or right hind, right fore, and so on. The training level tests ask only for a medium walk because at this level, the horse will not have the physical ability to carry himself in a correct collected walk; he will simply not have the strength to set himself back on his haunches without destroying the gait. In the medium walk, we ask only that the horse be equally balanced over all four legs.

To best understand riding the walk, let's discuss the walk at the beginning of any riding session. We enter the arena and begin our warm-up, almost always at the walk. It will not be surprising if the horse is a little stiff at this point, and this will be reflected in shorter steps and a tighter back. To ride the horse out of this and into a rhythmic and relaxed walk, we have to be able to feel the length of his stride, so that we can encourage his walk just enough to begin to stretch his walk stride. If we push too much, the horse will then begin taking short tight steps again, jig, or break into the trot. Ask your horse to move on at the walk just a little with the lower leg, and allow your seat to follow his movement. If we do not follow this movement with our seat, we will block the movement, but more often than not riders tend to push too much at the walk with their seat and end up inadvertently disrupting the horse's natural rhythm. Let your lower leg, not your seat, encourage the horse at this point. Concentrate on balancing on your pelvis in its neutral position and relaxing your thighs, so that you invite the movement to come through your legs and into the horse's neck.

When your horse is able to maintain this tempo, ask him for a little more, and so on until you have the best walk that you two can do at this time. You may want to experiment with just how much you can ask before his steps shorten again, or he breaks into the trot, so that you have a full understanding of the range of his walk. Thus you will not only know just how much you can ask for before things go wrong but also feel when his walk has improved over time.

While you are learning to feel your horse's stride under you, don't forget that you must give him his neck as well. Since the horse uses his neck to walk, ride with a longer rein than you would use for the trot or canter, and when you have even contact, be sure that your contact is passive and follows the horse's head, rather than restricting it.

The Free Walk

The free walk can be the most beautiful movement of all those in the training level tests. The horse comes out of the corner and heads diagonally across the arena. The reins slide effortlessly through the rider's hands as the horse stretches out his neck, his body elongates, and his strides widen. Relaxation and forward movement cause the muscles to ripple over his back, and he becomes as slinky and graceful as a panther. A beautiful free walk can be mesmerizing.

The key to a good walk on a loose rein is keeping the horse focused. A feeling of purpose or direction will give him the confidence to remain obedient and relaxed. When riding the walk on the loose rein, encourage the horse's hind legs to take large steps, his back to stretch and swing, and his neck to stretch down and out. Be careful not to let the horse curl; have the confidence to give your hands forward and offer him enough rein to stretch his neck out and forward in a way that will open his throatlatch. Remember that you are controlling his speed with your seat, and use the plastic figure, corridor, and force field concepts to keep him straight down the diagonal, so you don't hinder him from stretching out his neck by attempting to steer with the reins.

The Working Trot

The working trot is the bread-and-butter gait of training level. As the horse and rider progress up through the levels, it will still be used in the warm-up at the beginning of each work session and as a cool-down at the end, as it serves to relax the horse. The USEF defines it as a pace in which a lower-level horse "shows himself properly balanced and, remaining on the bit, goes forward with even, elastic steps and good hock action. The expression 'good hock action' does not mean that collection is a required quality of working trot. It only underlines the importance of an impulsion originated from the activity of the hindquarters."

We should also note that "properly balanced" means that the horse should have equal weight on all four legs, not that he should be set back on his haunches. And take note that "remaining on the bit" refers to an even connection between hind end and front end, so that the horse moves into the bridle. It does not mean that the rider should pull the horse's head down onto the vertical. In fact, think rather of pushing the neck out so that you can see the muscles along the top flexing.

The Twenty-Meter Circle in Working Trot
To properly ride a circle, think of the three images discussed in the molding aids section in part one: the corridor, the plastic Indian, and the force field. The reason these images can be helpful in steering a horse on the circle is that the knowledgeable rider steers her horse from the withers, or even from the haunches, not from the nose. Don't try to turn the horse by pointing his head in one direction or the other; remember, his legs come out of his body, not his head. Think, instead, of riding the horse as if you are pushing him in front of you (Mary Wanless's "pushing the baby buggy"), bending him with your seat and steering him through the withers. To turn to the left, accentuate the swing of your left, or inside, hip down and forward; your outside leg may drop back a little, but not too much, or the horse may think that you are about to ask for the canter. The inside leg asks the horse to move forward, holds the inside shoulder up, and begins the bending sequence; the outside leg catches the horse to keep him inside the corridor. Think of bending the horse around your strong

inside leg, almost as if it were planted like a pole in the sand, while you allow the inside hip to swing.

This can also feel as if you are twisting the horse between your legs, since the centrifugal force of moving on a circle or around a corner will force the horse against your outside leg, and you will have to apply an equal amount of pressure in return to contain the horse and to encourage the outside legs to take the necessary longer stride. Be careful not to be too active with your outside leg, however; if you push the horse over with your outside leg only, it will pivot on its hind end and lose engagement behind. A strong inside leg will ensure that the horse's inside hind steps up to take the weight, while the outside legs complete the turn.

To recap: on a circle or turn, the rider's inside leg keeps a horse from falling in on the circle, and her outside leg prevents the horse from veering out. If you focus on what is happening to the horse's body, and not his neck or nose, you will have an easier time putting him back on course in the middle of your corridor.

Many riders confuse the bending of the horse's neck to one side with true bend in the horse's body, a confusion that will cause trouble not only now, when turning or performing a twenty-meter circle, but even more so later in lateral movements such as the shoulder-in and leg yield. Humans being naturally hand-oriented, an inexperienced rider instinctively tries to turn a horse with the reins, but if you step back and look at the situation logically, you will see just how poorly this works. Say that you are on a twenty-meter circle, and the horse starts to veer to the outside. The hand-oriented rider instinctively tries to correct this with her inside hand. But although pulling on the inside rein pulls the horse's nose in, it cannot stop the withers and the rest of the horse's body from continuing to swing out. The horse will jackknife at the withers, like an out-of-control tractor-trailer, and continue to slide outward in the direction of its outside shoulder. In its milder form, this situation is often referred to as the horse throwing his outside shoulder; a more pronounced version will have you crabbing out of control across the arena—probably in the direction of the barn.

A horse that falls in on the circle is the flip side of the same coin. If you attempt to stop your horse from falling in by pulling on the outside rein, you will again cause him to fold up or jackknife, and fall in on the circle even more rapidly. By attempting to turn him with your hands, you create a weakness in the horse's neck that will affect far more than just how he turns on the circle.

The seat-oriented rider, on the other hand, understands that the force that drives the horse out of or into the circle comes from the horse's body, not his head. If you remain aware of the horse's body as a whole and use the corridor, plastic figure, and force field images, you will be able to turn your horse without this jackknife effect. The only real use for the reins in these situations is to keep the horse's neck and head in the middle of his chest.

The Stretching Circle in the Working Trot
The USEF rule book offers a one-sentence definition for stretching the frame: "The horse gradually takes the reins, stretching forward and downward with light contact, while maintaining balance, rhythm and tempo and quality of the gait." In order to appreciate this movement you must apply this definition to the horse's muscular system (see "The Circle of Muscles," in part 1 of this book). If the horse is to stretch over his topline, his hindquarters and neck must act much like the two ends of a suspension bridge, raising and stretching his back. As the hind legs step up and under the horse, they pull on the haunches and send the croup down; at the same time the down and forward movement of the neck acts as a pull forward over the withers. To ensure that the horse stretches through his entire topline, including over his neck, the rider must keep a light contact in the reins. Too much contact will contract the neck, interrupt

the horse's ability to come from behind, and lead to overflexion, but if there is no contact at all, and the horse simply sticks his nose out, there will be no insurance that the horse is continuing the stretch over the top of his neck.

Paul Belasik illuminates this difference with a simple demonstration that you can easily perform. While sitting at a desk or table, slowly lean forward and rest your chin on the edge of the table. Notice how straight, even hollow, your neck can be in the position. Now try it again, but this time slowly lean forward and rest your forehead on the table instead of your chin. You should instantly feel the stretch down through the back of your neck and into your back.

The position of the horse's head and neck influences the amount and type of stretch the horse will perform. At training level it is probably best to be familiar with two of these types of stretches. We can call the first type the training stretch. In your training stretch, you do not give much rein away, but instead simply ask the horse's poll to lower. This is the type of stretch Paul Belasik explains. In this stretch, the horse's throatlatch does not open, and he will be slightly behind the vertical. It is very important, however, that the horse be actively moving into the contact, and not simply curling and ducking behind it.

The second type of stretch we might call the competition stretch, the "stretchy circle" asked for in the tests. In performing the stretchy circle, we ask the horse to open his throatlatch, and to travel with his nose in front of the vertical. The rider should ask the horse to stretch his nose down to at least his knees, while maintaining bit contact.

While riding both of these kinds of stretches, remember to keep your body erect and balanced, and to keep the horse coming from behind so that his front end does not end up grinding down into the arena sand.

The Change of Rein in the Working Trot

Even if you are sitting to the trot and riding straight through a large field, you will still be riding a left- or right-rein trot, with a little flexion in the horse. The outside rein should act as the horse's security blanket: it should always be there for him. When patting him, always use the inside hand; in this way, you will be praising him with a pat and softening him with the release of the inside rein. Remember also that the inside leg is the driving leg. So when it comes to changing rein at the working trot, there is a little more happening than just a change of posting diagonal (see "The Rising Trot," in part 1, for more on the diagonal). There should also be a shift in your mind, accompanied by a slight change in bend in the horse. Try not to override this shift and push the horse's outside shoulder out, or throw away the inside rein; keep the horse relatively straight, with just a bit of flexion at the poll and a hint of bend. Putting it together, the sequence when changing rein at the trot is: Prepare the horse by half-halting; change your post; switch your driving leg; ask for a slight change in flexion at the poll, with the horse's neck contained by the outside rein; displace the rib cage slightly to the outside; and shift your mind so that you are now, even while continuing straight, prepared to turn in the opposite direction.

The Loop in the Working Trot

The various forms of the serpentine pattern test the horse's ability to make light and supple turns to both sides and easily change his bend, responding to a change of the rider's inside leg. They are thus extremely good at revealing how laterally even the horse is.

The loop at training level is the precursor to the full serpentine found in the first level tests. In the loop, however, the horse and rider pair are asked to come only ten meters off the long side, to the centerline, before returning to the track.

The line of travel is curved at every point in this movement. If you are on the left rein, for example, the line from F to X will bend slightly left from F to just before the quarter line and bend slightly right from just after the quarter line to just before X. Similarly, through the second half of the loop, the horse will travel on a slightly curved path to the right from just after X to just before the quarter line and on a slightly curved path to the left from just after the quarter line to just before M, with a change of bend ridden through the quarter line.

In a standard arena your path should pass through the quarter line at the V–L–P line in the first half and at the S–I–R line in the second half of the loop. In the small arena, your loop will be steeper, and thus a little harder to ride. You will also not have as clear a marker against which to sight your quarter lines.

The Trot/Canter Transition

Perhaps the first thing to be said about the trot/canter transition is that transitions from one gait to another are just that, not from one speed to another. The canter is not necessarily a faster gait than the trot, so don't get caught up in pushing the horse forward into the transition. Think instead of lifting him into canter.

To ask for a canter strike-off to the right, the rider moves her left leg a few inches farther back than the right leg, which is directly under the rider's hip, near the girth. Moving the left leg back gives the signal to the horse's outside hind to start the canter sequence, while at the same time, the right hip is brought forward. Her right leg should simultaneously exert pressure equal to that of the left, and her upper body should be kept steady and not twisted. At this point think of turning on your beacon (see fig. 4) and projecting your center of gravity, not your shoulders, forward.

Because it is important that the horse learn to come under the rider's weight when striking off by engaging his hind legs under him, rather than throwing his head up to shift his weight back, it may be necessary to flex the horse slightly to the inside with the right rein or ask for a slight shoulder fore. But keep in mind that it is very important at this stage to make the canter strike-off as straight as possible; do not overuse the inside rein, and do not use the outside leg too strongly, since this will push the hindquarters sideways. If you are not careful about this now, you will find it extremely difficult to achieve straight tempi changes later, without your horse fishtailing back and forth with each change.

There are many who advocate asking for the canter with the outside leg; the horse's outside hind leg does initiate the canter sequence, after all. However, concentrating too much on one aspect of the canter depart, whether it be inside or outside leg aid, can imbalance both horse and rider. Think more of encouraging a lift into the canter; keep the horse's motion even from back to front, and try not to let the energy run forward through your hands, instead of aiding in the lifting of the horse's withers. At this point, use both legs evenly when asking for the canter; and in particular, both calves. Remember that when the rider moves her outside leg back, she also increases the weight on her inside seat bone slightly. An easy way to understand this is to simply stand with both feet firmly on the ground, then move one leg back slightly. To do this, you must place all of your weight on the other leg so you can lift the first leg off the ground and move it back. A similar event takes place in the saddle; moving one leg back a little happens simultaneously with a little more weight in the opposite seat bone. Once this correlation between the outside leg and inside seat bone has been made clear to the horse, he will then begin to make the connection between pressure from the inside seat bone and the request for canter.

Let's go through this again, step by step, from the posting trot. After establishing a relaxed and even trot, go to the sitting trot for a stride or two. Now you are in position to ask for the canter, and the horse has just gotten a heads-up that something is about to happen. Half-halt to make it clear to the horse that you are about to ask for something. Then slide your outside leg back behind the girth while your inside hip moves slightly forward, putting a little weight in your inside seat bone and stirrup. Begin by giving a squeeze with both thighs, or even better both calves, but bear in mind that eventually you will want to ask for the canter with only the inside seat bone!

The Twenty-Meter Circle in Working Canter
The canter is a three-beat gait. The right lead canter, for example, is initiated by the left hind leg, followed by the right hind and left fore hitting the ground simultaneously for the second beat, and finally by the right fore, which lands alone. This is followed by a moment of suspension, after which the sequence repeats.

Okay, what do we do with that? Well, for now, perhaps nothing much, but you will use this information later in your riding. At this point, there are a few other things to keep in mind when riding the canter on the circle.

Riding the canter requires some coordination of your leg and core muscles. To properly ride the canter, the rider must learn to keep her seat in the saddle and think of scooping the horse up into the canter stride. The rider's core muscles should create a forward and upward push. If they do not, then the rider's seat will leave the back of the saddle with each canter stride; just when she is asking the horse to leap forward in the canter stride, her seat is heading out in the opposite direction! Thus the first order of business is to sit down into the saddle for the canter.

Once we are deep in the saddle, we can influence the horse's forward push by using a combination of stomach and leg muscles to lift the horse up into each stride. And here is our real focus in riding the canter, not pulling the horse up with our hands. Riding the canter from the seat asks the horse to use himself; using the hands asks him to come on the forehand.

Riding the canter this way may mean only a slight flexing and relaxing of the stomach and leg muscles, thereby placing a little more weight on the seat bones, to keep the canter going when all is well, or it may require a strong squeeze and scoop to bring the horse into a better canter or prevent him from breaking into the trot. But however much pressure the rider needs, the seat and leg tone scoop the horse into the stride and then relax, then scoop again, then relax, and so on, in keeping with the rhythm of the canter. With this in mind, we come to the expression, "Breathing with your thighs," which is just another version of "The release of the aid is the aid." By breathing with your thighs, you will also give yourself the chance to keep your legs long.

Be careful also to keep your seat and leg aids independent from your upper body. If you are not careful about keeping your upper body still, you will most likely end up throwing your inside shoulder forward with every canter stride, unfortunately an all too common sight. Think instead of being the swan. All the work takes place under the waterline, while above the water, the swan glides gracefully along.

Finally, use the plastic figure, corridor, and force field concepts in the canter as well to keep your horse on the circle.

The Canter/Trot Transition

Remember: all down transitions are forward in their thought and execution. The horse cannot be allowed to shift down by running up against the reins, as this will only throw him on his forehand. When a horse travels on his forehand, he is unable to muster the proper pushing power from behind; this can also lead to back injury, as he will be less able to carry the rider's weight.

A large part of a good transition from the canter to the trot is having a canter that is balanced and relaxed; a down transition can only be as good as the gait that precedes it. After picking up the canter and establishing good rhythm and balance, prepare the horse for the down transition by giving him a half-halt to let him know that something is up. Now half-halt again, but this time hold it so that he transitions down to the trot. If you have to back up the inside leg, use your outside rein just a bit. Remember also that you will have to engage your core muscles so as not to pitch forward, then begin your rising trot to carry you through the motion.

An important aspect of any down transition is that you do not lose the tempo from one gait to the other; though the gait changes, your tempo shouldn't. In preparing for your transition, remember to bring the canter to a tempo that you will be able to maintain in the trot. At rising trot this shouldn't be too hard, but once you begin to sit to the trot you may find yourself unable at first to keep up with the trot following a strong canter. Remember also that as the release of the aid is the aid, you should not wait for the horse to come down to the trot before positioning yourself to ride the trot. If this transition is to be smooth, you must remember that the transition from canter to trot is one between two gaits, not two speeds, so you will not want the horse to halt or slow while moving from canter to trot. As soon as you give the down transition aid, you will need to be ready to push the horse into the trot.

The Corners

There are two issues to think of when riding the corners. First, riding the corners in either trot or canter is like riding part of a very small circle, so that much of what is happening with the horse and rider is similar to what happens in the twenty-meter circle. As the horse's strength and balance improve, he will be able to go deeper into the corner, but still think of this as riding part of an ever smaller circle. Second, be sure that you are actually riding the corner. If you just sit on a horse and point him down the long side, he will "turn a corner" simply because there is a wall or rail in front of him. This is not the same as riding the corner. It is a useful diagnostic to occasionally turn a few strides before the corner made by the arena rail, to check whether you are truly positioning the horse in this movement.

The horse will need to work a little harder to move through a corner properly. This is because the turn puts more stress on his inside hind leg. If you walk in a small circle, you will notice that your inside leg needs to take more of your body's weight, while your outside leg swings around and takes a longer stride. The smaller the circle you walk, the more weight you put on your inside leg and the longer the stride of the outside leg. When you add speed to this equation, you bring to the picture centrifugal force, which pulls you off the load-bearing inside leg.

Think of a car racing around a corner. When the car begins its turn, it is redirecting the forward momentum that it had coming into the corner. This forward momentum now acts as a hindrance to the car as it tries to turn. If the car turns too sharply, or if you put on the brakes, the power of the forward momentum will lift the inside wheels of the car and send it toppling over in the direction of the original forward movement.

When moving into and through a corner, the horse must have enough strength to resist this force that is trying to pull it off of its load-bearing inside leg, which is why the corner should only be ridden as deep as the horse is strong enough to handle.

Because there is more work involved for the horse in riding a corner, he will often slow down a little there. Since our very first concern is to establish rhythm, we must be sure to ask for a little more effort from the horse in the corners, to combat this. To return to the car analogy, when we approach a turn while driving, we first put on the brakes to slow the car down to a manageable speed. After we have entered the turn, we can then press on the gas to accelerate while in the turn, for a smoother drive. A similar situation arises when we ride a horse into a corner. Make sure that your tempo down the long side is one that you will be able to keep in the corner. Give your horse a heads-up just before entering the corner, then ride through it, asking the horse for a little more effort so that he maintains the original tempo.

The Halt; or, The Trot/Walk/Halt Transition

All down transitions are forward in their thought and execution. The chief aim of the transition is not to let the horse decelerate by leaning into the reins and breaking his forward momentum with stiffening forelegs, which is akin to a car hitting a low wall, crunching its front end down, and having its back end soar up into the air and flip over. A poorly performed halt will throw the horse on his forehand, and in many cases cause his haunches to veer to one side. That is why, in the training level tests, halts may be made through the walk. If we keep the horse moving forward through the downward transitions, it is easier to ensure that his hind legs stay engaged and play an active role in rebalancing him during deceleration. Over time more weight will shift to the hind legs as the horse is rebalanced, but at this point we are just looking for keeping the horse off his forelegs.

The key, then, to a proper trot/walk/halt transition lies in stabilizing your body. When you ride the trot, your body is moving in the rhythm of the horse's movement. Just before asking for the transition, sit one or two strides in the trot, while continuing to follow the movement over the horse's back. This change from rising to sitting trot will also act as a heads-up to the horse that something is about to happen. Once you have sat to the trot, you can now activate your core muscles and breathe out a long, drawn-out breath to influence the movement over the horse's back, slowing the horse down to a walk and then to a halt. By activating your core muscles, you will keep your torso vertical and strong so that you do not end up tipping forward or leaning backward. Remember also not to hollow or round your back and to keep your seat down on the saddle. Essentially, the halt aid is stopping the movement of your seat bones—Mary Wanless uses the image of dampening your movement on a trampoline—while keeping your torso properly balanced over the horse.

It is very important that your hands do not pull back, but offer only a passive resistance. Halt the horse with your seat, using your hands only as a passive wall that the horse will come up against if he persists. An image that may help is to think of pushing the horse into the circle of your hips, arms, and reins. The horse cannot go out of this circle, either by blowing through your hands or by dragging behind, which would cause him to land on his forehand. At the moment that you are engaging your stomach muscles to slow and then halt the horse, you should also give a slight squeeze with the inside leg. This pressure helps bring the horse up into the down transition. Again, as the release of the aid is the aid; do not hold the pressure, or you will block the last step into the halt. In fact, release it even before the horse fully makes the transition. Think of it as two almost simultaneous movements: the blocking seat and activating leg that brings the horse down and the release that allows the horse to come forward into the halt.

To recap: Pick up a rising trot, making sure that the horse is relaxed and has a slight flexion to the inside. To initiate the trot/walk/halt transition, sit to the trot, keep your core muscles strong and your torso balanced over the horse, breathe out a long breath, engage your back and abdominal muscles to block the horse's movement over its back (think closing down on the horse), keep your legs along his flank, and squeeze with the inside calf to encourage his back legs to step forward and under him and to place him inside your hip/arm/rein circle. Then at the very end release the leg pressure a little to allow the horse to move into the halt. Don't wait for him to halt before releasing the pressure. The release of the aid allows him to finish the halt. If he does not finish it, correct him. If he does, praise him.

The Tests, Movement by Movement

Dressage is a mental, as well as physical, sport. Hopefully, you have learned something of the complexity of training level by reading this book. But the principals set forth in these pages, the fundamentals of dressage riding, must constantly be applied and evaluated each stride of your ride. We must be constantly taking in the information from our bodies, our horses, and our surroundings, constantly evaluating this information through the filter of correct fundamentals, and developing strategies based on these diagnostics in order to create a beautiful and healthy horse.

With this in mind, I have written below a narrative of some of what might be going through a rider's mind while performing each of the training level tests.

The repetition in these comments is meant to bring to the rider's attention two ideas. The first is that you must actively ride every movement in these tests: just because you have gone through in your mind what it will take to correctly ride through one corner, for example, that doesn't mean that you can approach the next corner any less actively. The second is that you as the rider must constantly reevaluate your situation. You may find that you need to correct or support your horse differently in different parts of the test: a trot corner to the left may need to be ridden differently than a trot corner to the right, and so on. The more actively engaged you are in reevaluating and riding each movement of your test, the more successful a ride you will have.

And by successful, I mean that by feeling, listening to your horse, collecting as much data as you can, and then evaluating it and acting on it, you will learn more about how to ride correctly and beautifully. As a byproduct of this, your scores will rise. You may see this through the course of one test, or it may take a longer period. But through listening, feeling, discipline, and practice you will gain a deeper understanding of riding, a better appreciation of your horse, and an improvement in your scores.

2011 Training Level Test 1

Before entering, let your horse trot past the judge's booth in both directions. Be aware that he may find this spooky, but don't give him the idea that he should be worried about the judge. As you approach the judge's box, look over to the other side of the arena and plan where you will turn around to pass by the judge's box again. Let the horse see the box from both sides, but don't let him know that is what you are doing.

As you make your approach to enter the arena at A, look up at the judge, find X by checking B and E, and draw a line in the sand with your eyes back from X along the centerline to you and your horse as you enter. Have both force fields at the ready to keep your horse on the centerline. Before X half-halt, then ask for the down transition, releasing your aid so he comes forward into the walk. Half-halt again, and then ask for a halt. Salute.

Keep your eyes up while you ask the horse to move on at the walk and then at the trot. Mentally prepare yourself for the trot transition; go through your checklist of how you will ask and release, how you will keep your upper body quiet and balanced over your hips and not leaning forward, and how you will dictate the tempo with your posting, using the metronome concept. Don't get ahead of the horse, and don't fall behind. As you proceed toward C, keep your corridor walls strong and your force field at the ready.

As you approach C, half-halt your horse, allow him to feel your right corridor wall, and begin to open your left hip swing to invite him to track left.

Before making your turn at C, look over to H and draw a line back through the corner and to you. Decide how deep you will go into the corner based on your horse's balance and your ability to support him. As you ride through the corner, look down the rail toward E. As you approach E, half-halt your horse to let him know that something is about to happen. Then allow him to feel your outside (right) corridor wall and open your inside hip swing to lead him onto the twenty-meter circle. Keep your eyes up and begin drawing your lines and playing back your video, first from the centerline back to E, then from B back to the centerline, then from the centerline of the second half of the circle back to B, and finally from E again back to the centerline, so that you both plan your route and are led by it. As you approach E, allow the horse to feel your inside (left) corridor wall to prepare him to continue down the rail. Then look down to your corner and plan your route through it, based on your horse's balance and your ability to support him. As you trot through the corner, look at A.

As you approach A, find your four points of the circle and let your eyes play back each quarter or half circle as you make your circle. As you approach the centerline, have in your mind where you will take the canter. If your horse is slow to respond, start the process soon after crossing the centerline; if your horse is quick off the aid or feels tense, pick an area closer to the rail, wait until you have crossed the centerline, then calmly ask for the canter. To ask for the canter, remember to sit to the trot, half-halt, and then take the canter; keep your shoulders back, sit into the canter, and let your belly button lead.

As you take the canter, look up and begin delineating your path from A, through the corner, and on to F. Have in mind how far into the corner you hope to ride as you approach A. Then, as you ride through the corner, look down the rail toward B.

While approaching B, begin playing back the half circle in your mind. Regulate the horse between your corridor walls. As you cross the centerline, look forward toward E and on down the rail toward V or K.

While approaching E, look ahead and envision your transition to trot in the center of the space between E and K. If your horse is slow to respond, begin preparing as you pass E; if he is quick, wait to pass E first. Remember the half-halt to regulate and balance the canter before the transition. As you come down to trot, look ahead to the corner and plan how deep you will be able to go into it. Make your video. Through the corner, prepare yourself and the horse for the stretchy circle at A by keeping him balanced and regulating his trot tempo.

As you approach A, keep your eyes up and play back each quarter or half circle in your mind as you ride the stretchy circle. Make sure to give the horse enough rein to allow him to put his nose below his knee, and to keep his throatlatch open. Not giving him enough rein will simply make him curl. Regulate his trot and his circle with your corridor walls. As you approach A again and begin to take up the reins, mentally prepare yourself for the upcoming transition to walk. Half-halt the horse to alert him to the coming transition.

As you approach A again, decide where between A and F you will make your transition, and how deeply your horse's balance will allow you to go into the corner. Make your transition where you will still have time afterward to prepare him for turning onto the diagonal and the free walk at F. You have already half-halted to alert him that something is about to happen. Now half-halt again and this time finish it off into a down transition. Elongate the front of your torso as you make your transition. After the transition prepare your horse for the turn onto the diagonal at F while your eyes begin to play back the line from H.

Activate your corridor walls to straighten your horse at F and prepare your force field in case he tries to stray along the diagonal to H. Eyes up. Hands forward. Think purpose. Don't pump with your seat if you feel he needs to be more forward; give him a little leg aid and release. Just before H, keep him straight with your legs as you gather up the reins, while your eyes draw your line through the corner and over to C. Actively ride your corner; that is, determine ahead of time how deep you and your horse can go without compromising your gait.

Before C, mentally prepare yourself for the trot transition; go through your checklist of how you will ask and release, how you will keep your upper body quiet and balanced over your hips and not leaning forward, and how your posting will set the tempo. Don't get ahead of the horse, and don't fall behind. The transition is at C, meaning when your leg is next to the letter. If your horse is slow to the aids, you may need to half-halt to get his attention; if he is quick, remember to keep your aids quiet and more subtle. As you transition to trot, look ahead to the corner and draw your line through it based on your horse's balance, then look down the rail to B. Just before B, half-halt your horse or two to let him know that something is about to happen. As you approach B, let him feel your outside leg and begin to open the swing of your inside hip.

Strengthen your outside corridor wall and activate your outside force field as your inside hip invites the horse onto the circle at B. As you enter the circle, use your video to begin drawing lines back and forth from the centerline to B, from E to the centerline, from the centerline on the second half of the circle back to E, and from B back to the centerline, so that you both determine your path and are drawn by it. Use your corridor walls and force field to keep the horse on your path. As you approach B again, look down the rail toward F and allow your horse to feel the inside corridor wall that will now hold him to the rail. Have your inside force field at the ready. As your trot down the rail, look toward A and begin mentally preparing for your circle and canter depart. How much time will you need to take the canter on the second half of the circle? How will this affect where you use your aids?

As you approach A, half-halt your horse and allow him to feel the outside corridor wall as you prepare, and then actually ride, the turn onto the circle at A. At the same time, keep your eyes up and begin your playback of the circle. Find your point on the rail and play it back to A, then look to the centerline and play that back to the rail. Prepare the second half of the circle during this second arc so that you will be able to concentrate more on your canter depart while you are on the second half of the circle. Decide ahead of time where you will take your canter. Decide how much preparation your horse will need. Remember to keep your head up, shoulders back, sit into the canter, and let your belly button lead.

Now look to A and on to the corner before K and draw your line. Prepare your horse for the corner and look down the rail toward E.

While approaching E, begin playing back the half circle in your mind; regulate the horse between your corridor walls. As you cross the centerline, look forward toward B and on down the rail toward P or F.

While approaching B, look ahead and envision your transition to trot in the center of the space between B and F. If your horse is slow to the aids, begin preparing as you pass B; if he is quick, wait to pass B first. Remember the half-halt to regulate the canter before the transition. As you are transitioning to trot, look ahead to the corner and plan how deeply you will be able to go into it, based on your horse's balance and your ability to support him. Find your line in the sand and continue drawing it over toward A and down the centerline. Prepare mentally to guide your horse through two turns in rapid succession. As you enter your corner, begin looking down the centerline and allow your horse to feel your outside corridor wall so that he will be better prepared to turn onto the centerline. Your line through these two corners should not compromise his balance or slow his tempo, but you cannot allow him to overshoot the centerline. Prepare his balance and regulate his tempo before the corner.

As you strengthen your outside corridor wall, keep your force field at the ready, and look down the centerline at the judge, prepare to soften your outside wall (left) and strengthen your inside (right) corridor so that the horse travels straight down the centerline. Have both force fields at the ready to keep him straight toward X as you use your video playback to draw your line. Before X half-halt, then ask for a down transition, and release so he comes forward down into a walk. Half-halt again, and then ask for a halt. Salute. Speak to the judge only when spoken to; otherwise, leave the arena at a walk on a long rein by continuing up to C, turning along the rail, and exiting at A.

2011 Training Level Test 2
Before entering, let your horse trot by the judge's booth in both directions. Be aware that he may find this spooky, but don't give him the idea that he should be worried about the judge. As you approach the judge's box, look over to the other side of the arena and plan where you will turn around to pass by the judge's box again. Let the horse see the box from both sides, but don't let him know that is what you are doing.

As you make your approach to enter the arena at A, look up at the judge, find X by checking B and E, and draw a line in the sand with your eyes back from X along the centerline to you and your horse as you enter. Have both force fields at the ready to keep your horse on the centerline. Before X half-halt, then ask for the down transition, releasing your aid so he comes forward into the walk. Half-halt again, and then ask for a halt. Salute.

Keep your eyes up while you ask the horse to move on at the walk and then at the trot. Mentally prepare yourself for the trot transition; go through your checklist of how you will ask and release, how you will keep your upper body quiet and balanced over your hips and not leaning forward, and how you will dictate the tempo with your posting, using the metronome concept. Don't get ahead of the horse, and don't fall behind. As you proceed toward C, keep your corridor walls strong and your force field at the ready.

As you approach C, half-halt your horse, allow him to feel your left corridor wall, and begin to open your right hip swing to invite him to track right.

Before making your turn at C, look over to M and draw a line back through the corner and to you. Decide how deep you will go into the corner based on your horse's balance and your ability to support him. As you ride through the corner, look down the rail toward B. As you approach B, half-halt your horse to let him know that something is about to happen. Then allow him to feel your outside (left) corridor wall and open your inside hip swing to lead him onto the circle. Keep your eyes up and begin drawing your lines and playing back your video, first from the centerline back to B, then from E back to the centerline, then from the centerline of the second half of the circle back to E, and finally from B again back to the centerline, so that you both plan your route and are led by it. As you approach B again, allow the horse to feel your inside (right) corridor wall to prepare him to continue down the rail. Then look down to your corner and plan your route through it, based on your horse's balance and your ability to support him. As you trot through the corner, look over to the next corner and plan your route through it. Remember that shortly after trotting through this second corner you will need to be prepared to take your horse onto the diagonal at K. As you come out of the circle and approach K, half-halt your horse and allow him to feel your outside corridor wall so that he understands that a turn is coming.

As you bring your horse onto the diagonal at K, look across the arena to M and trace your line back to you. Go over this line a few times as you ride your diagonal. Keep your corridor walls strong and your force field at the ready to keep the horse on track. Wait until a few strides before M to change your posting diagonal. This both minimizes the chance of you unbalancing your horse across the diagonal and gives him a natural half-halt as you approach the rail. Allow him to feel your inside (left) corridor wall to hold him onto the rail at M. As you are changing your posting diagonal and asking the horse to remain on the rail, draw your line through the corner to C and back to you. Decide what path you will take based on your horse's balance and your ability to support him. Let your eyes draw this line back and forth between you and C so as to both set your course and lead you through it. As you approach C, determine where between C and H you will take your canter depart.

As you approach C and decide where you will take your canter depart, keep in mind whether your horse is slow to the aids, in which case you may want to start asking as you cross C, or quick to the aids, in which case you may want to wait until you are definitely past C. Remember in the canter depart to keep your head up, shoulders back, sit into the canter, and let your belly button lead. As you canter through your corner, look down the rail toward E. Just before E, half-halt your horse and allow him to feel your outside (right) corridor wall.

As you give your half-halt and ready your horse for the turn onto the circle, begin drawing your back-and-forth arc lines. First find your point on the centerline and draw a line in the sand back to you at E, then look at B and draw your line back to the centerline, then to the centerline of the second half of the circle back to B, and finally from E again back to the centerline. Draw this line back and forth a number of times to reinforce your path. As you complete your circle and approach E, give the half-halt and allow him to feel your inside (left) corridor wall as you look down the rail and prepare for your down transition between E and K.

While approaching E, look ahead and envision your transition to trot in the center of the space between E and K; if you are riding in a standard arena, this will be at V. If your horse is slow to the aids, begin preparing as you pass E; if he is quick, wait to pass E first. Remember the half-halt to regulate the canter before the transition. As you are transitioning to trot, open and strengthen your front, look ahead to the corner, and plan how deep you will be able to go. Make your video. Through the corner, prepare yourself and the horse for the stretchy circle at A by keeping him balanced and regulating his trot tempo.

As you approach A, keep your eyes up and play back each quarter or half circle in your mind as you ride the stretchy circle. Make sure to give the horse enough rein to allow him to put his nose below his knee and keep his throatlatch open. If you do not give him enough rein, he will simply curl. Regulate his trot tempo with your posting and his path with your corridor walls. As you approach A again and begin to take up the reins, mentally prepare yourself for the upcoming transition to walk. Half-halt to alert your horse to the coming transition.

As you approach A, decide where between A and F you will make your transition, and how deep into the corner your horse's balance will allow you to go. Make your transition where you will still have time afterward to prepare him for turning onto the diagonal and the free walk at F. You have already half-halted to alert him that something is about to happen. Now half-halt again, and this time finish it off into a down transition. Remember to give the aid for the transition to walk and then release it so that he is able to come forward into the walk. Elongate the front of your torso as you make your transition. After the transition prepare your horse for the turn onto the diagonal at F while your eyes begin to play back the line from H.

Activate your corridor walls to straighten your horse at F and ready your force field in case he tries to stray along the diagonal. Eyes up. Hands forward. Think purpose. Don't pump with your seat; if you feel he needs to be more forward, give him a little leg aid and release. Just before X, allow him to feel your left corridor wall as you look over to M. As you pass through X increase the pressure from the left corridor wall to turn him onto the new diagonal toward M. Be prepared to relax this left corridor wall and increase the pressure of the right corridor wall so that he does not turn too much. Gently catch him with your right leg and then gently nudge him off it to continue straight on his own toward M. Just before M, keep him straight with your legs as you gather up the reins while your eyes draw your line through the corner and over to C. Actively ride your corner; that is, determine ahead of time how deeply you and your horse can go into it without compromising your gait. As you ride through your corner, mentally prepare yourself for the trot transition.

Before C, mentally prepare yourself for the trot transition; go through your checklist of how you will ask and release, how you will keep your upper body quiet and balanced over your hips and not leaning forward, and how you will set the tempo with your posting. Don't get ahead of the horse and don't fall behind. The transition is at C, meaning when your girth is next to the letter. If your horse is slow to the aids, you may need to half-halt a few times to get his attention; if he is quick, remember to keep your aids quiet and more subtle. As you transition to trot, look ahead to the corner and draw your line through it based on your horse's balance, then look down the rail to E. Just before E, half-halt once or twice tolet him know that something is about to happen. As you approach E, let him feel your outside leg and begin to open the swing of your inside hip.

Strengthen your outside corridor wall and activate your outside force field as your inside hip invites the horse onto the circle at E. As you enter the circle, use your video to begin drawing lines back and forth from the centerline to E, from B to the centerline, from the centerline on the second half of the circle back to B, and from E back to the centerline, so that you both determine your path and are drawn by it. Use your corridor walls and force field to keep the horse on your path. As you approach E again, look down the rail toward K and allow your horse to feel the inside corridor wall that will now hold him to the rail. Have your inside force field at the ready. As your trot down the rail, look toward A and then draw a line back through the corner toward you. Once you have determined your corner path, look over toward F and draw a line through that corner toward A. As you approach this corner, mentally prepare yourself for the turn onto the diagonal at F, and shortly before F half-halt your horse and allow him to feel your outside (right) corridor wall.

As your bring your horse onto the diagonal at F, look across the arena to H and trace a line back to you. Go over this line a few times as you ride your diagonal. Keep your corridor walls strong and your force field at the ready to hold the horse on track. Wait until a few strides before H to change your posting diagonal. This both minimizes the chance of you unbalancing your horse across the diagonal and gives him a natural half-halt as you approach the rail. Allow him to feel your inside (left) corridor wall to hold him onto the rail at H. As you are changing your posting diagonal and asking the horse to remain on the rail, draw your line from C through the corner and back to you. Decide what path you will take based on your horse's balance and your ability to support him. Let your eyes draw this line back and forth between you and C so as to both set your course and lead you through it. As you approach C, determine where between C and M you will take your canter depart.

As you approach C and decide where you will take your canter depart, keep in mind whether your horse is slow to the aids, in which case you may want to start asking as you cross C, or quick to the aids, in which case you may want to wait until you are definitely past C. Remember in the canter depart to keep your head up and your shoulders back, sit into the canter, and let your belly button lead. As you canter through your corner, look down the rail toward B. Just before B, half-halt your horse and allow him to feel your outside (left) corridor wall.

As you half-halt and ready your horse for the turn onto the circle, begin drawing your back-and-forth arc lines. First find your point on the centerline and draw a line in the sand back to you at B, then look at E and draw your line back to the centerline, then to the centerline of the second half of the circle back to E, and finally from B again back to the centerline. Draw this line back and forth a number of times to reinforce your path. As you complete your circle and approach B again, half-halt your horse and allow him to feel your inside (right) corridor wall as you look down the rail and prepare for your down transition between B and F.

While approaching B, look ahead and envision your transition to trot in the center of the space between B and F. If your horse is slow to the aids, begin preparing as you pass B; if he is quick, wait to pass B first. Remember the half-halt to regulate the canter before your transition. As you make the transition to trot, look ahead to the corner and plan how deeply you will be able to go into it. Make your video. Through the corner, prepare yourself and your horse for the turn down the centerline at A by keeping him balanced and regulating his trot tempo with your posting.

As you strengthen your outside corridor wall and keep your force field at the ready while looking down the centerline at the judge, prepare to soften your outside wall (left) and strengthen your inside (right) corridor so that the horse travels straight down the centerline. Have both force fields at the ready to keep him straight toward X as you use your video playback to draw your line. Before X half-halt and then ask and release to have him come forward down into a walk. Half-halt again and then ask for a halt. Salute. Speak to the judge only when spoken to; otherwise, leave the arena at a walk on a long rein by continuing up to C, turning along the rail, and exiting at A.

2011 Training Level Test 3
Before entering, let your horse trot by the judge's booth in both directions. Be aware that he may find this spooky, but don't give him the idea that he should be worried about the judge. As you approach the judge's box, look over to the other side of the arena and plan where you will turn around to pass by the judge's box again. Let the horse see the box from both sides, but don't let him know that is what you are doing.

As you make your approach to enter the arena at A, look up at the judge, find X by checking B and E, and draw a line in the sand with your eyes back from X along the centerline as you and your horse enter. Have both force fields at the ready to keep your horse on the centerline. Before X half-halt, then ask for the down transition, releasing your aid so he comes forward into the walk. Half-halt again, and then ask for a halt. Salute.

Keep your eyes up while you ask the horse to move on at the walk and then at the trot. Mentally prepare yourself for the trot transition; go through your checklist of how you will ask and release, how you will keep your upper body quiet and balanced over your hips and not lean forward, and how you will dictate the tempo with your posting, using the metronome concept. Don't get ahead of the horse, and don't fall behind. As you proceed toward C, keep your corridor walls strong and your force field at the ready.

As you approach C, half-halt your horse, allow him to feel your left corridor wall, and begin to open your right hip swing to invite him to track right.

Before making your turn at C, look over to H and draw a line back through the corner and to you. Decide how deeply you will ride into the corner based on your horse's balance and your ability to support him; keep in mind also that you will be coming off the rail at H to start the first part of your loop. As you ride through the corner, look into the arena and find X. As you half-halt your horse and allow him to feel your outside (right) corridor wall to begin your loop, draw your curved line from X back to you at H, planning where you will change bend as you cross the quarter line. Keep your corridor walls strong and your force field at the ready in order to guide your horse along this curved line. Look down at K and draw the second curved line of the loop, the one between X and K, again planning where you will smoothly change bend at the quarter line. As you approach X, look over to A and draw your line back through the corner to

K. Decide how deeply you will ride into the corner, based on your horse's balance and your ability to support him. As you ride through your corner, look over to A and mentally prepare for your canter depart.

As you approach A and decide where you will take your canter depart, keep in mind whether your horse is slow to the aids, in which case you may want to start asking as you cross A, or quick to the aids, in which case you may want to wait until you are definitely past A. Remember in the canter depart to keep your head up and your shoulders back, to sit into the canter, and to let your belly button lead. As you canter through your corner, look down the rail toward B. Just before B, half-halt your horse and allow him to feel your outside (right) corridor wall.

As you half-halt and ready your horse for the turn onto the circle, begin drawing your back-and-forth arc lines. First find your point on the centerline and draw a line in the sand back to you at B, then look at E and draw your line back to the centerline, then to the centerline of the second half of the circle back to E, and finally from B again back to the centerline. Draw this line back and forth a number of times to reinforce your path. As you complete your circle and approach B, half-halt your horse and allow him to feel your inside (left) corridor wall as you look down the rail toward the corner between M and C. As you make your way down the rail, draw your line from C back through the corner and to yourself. Decide how deeply into the corner you will go, depending on your horse's balance and your ability to support him. As you ride this corner, look over to the next corner between C and H. Draw your line from H back through the corner to C. Again, keep in mind your and your horse's ability in deciding how far into the corner to ride. Keep in mind also that you will be turning onto the diagonal at H, and that you and your horse will need to work a little extra to make those turns back to back. As you approach H, half-halt your horse and allow him to feel your outside (right) corridor wall to prepare him for the turn onto the diagonal.

As you bring your horse onto the diagonal at H, ready your left corridor wall and force field to catch and then gently nudge your horse if need be to ask him to continue straight along the diagonal himself. At the same time, look across the arena to F and trace your line back to you. Go over this line a few times as you ride your diagonal. Keep your corridor walls strong and your force field at the ready to hold the horse on track. Now find X and prepare for your down transition to the trot, mentally going over your down transition aids. How does your horse feel at this moment? Will he need lighter or stronger aids to come down? Add this information on your horse to your preparation. Just before X, half-halt your horse both to regulate the canter and to give him a heads-up, then follow through with a down transition. As you make the transition to trot, open and strengthen your front, prepare to regulate the trot tempo with your posting if necessary, and look up toward F to keep straight on the diagonal. As you approach F, draw your line from A back through the corner toward F. Decide how deeply into the corner you will ride, based on your horse's balance and your ability to support him. As you enter the corner, look over to A and begin mentally preparing for the walk transition.

As you are riding the second half of the corner between F and A, with your eye on A, having mentally prepared your down transition, half-halt your horse and then follow through with a transition. Remember to give the aid for the transition to walk and then release it so that he is able to come forward into the walk. Open and strengthen the front of your torso as you make your transition. Keep in mind also that this transition is at the letter, so you will want your girth at A when you ride into the medium walk. As you are transitioning, look up toward K and draw your line back through the corner toward you. Keep in mind your horse's balance, the quality of his trot, and your ability at that moment to support him when deciding your path through the corner. As you ride into the corner, mentally prepare yourself for turning onto the diagonal at K and go over your aids for the free walk.

Activate your corridor walls to straighten your horse at K, and have your force field at the ready in case he tries to stray along the diagonal. Eyes up. Hands forward. Think purpose. Don't pump with your seat; if you feel he needs to be more forward, give him a little leg aid and release. Just before X, allow him to feel your left corridor wall as you look over to H. As you pass through X, increase the pressure from the left corridor wall to turn him onto the new diagonal toward H. Be prepared to relax this left corridor wall and increase the pressure of the right corridor wall so that he does not turn too much. Gently catch him with your right leg and then nudge him off it to continue straight on his own toward H. Just before H, keep him straight with your legs as you gather up the reins while your eyes draw your line from C back through the corner. Actively ride your corner; that is, determine ahead of time how deeply into it you and your horse can go without compromising your gait. As you ride through your corner, mentally prepare yourself for the trot transition.

Before making your turn at C, look over to M and draw a line back through the corner and to you. Decide how deeply into the corner you will go, based on your horse's balance and your ability to support him; keep in mind also that you will be coming off the rail at M to start the first part of your loop. As you ride through the corner, look into the arena and find X. As you half-halt your horse and allow him to feel your left corridor wall to begin your loop, draw your curved line from X back to you at M. Keep your corridor walls strong and your force field at the ready in order to guide your horse on this curved line, and look down at F and draw the second curved line of the loop, the one between X and F, so that you will have planned where you want to be when you start your change of bend through X. As you approach X, gradually begin to straighten your horse by allowing him to now feel your left corridor wall a little, so that as you pass through X you are straight on the centerline. As you pass through X, strengthen your left corridor wall to continue the change in bend, while simultaneously adding pressure to your right corridor wall to direct the horse onto his new curve. As you do this draw this line in your mind from F back to X. As you approach X, look over to A and draw your line back through the corner to F. Decide how deep you will go in the corner based on your horse's balance and your ability to support him. As you ride through your corner, look over to A and mentally prepare for your canter depart.

As you approach A and decide where you will take your canter depart, keep in mind whether your horse is slow to the aids, in which case you may want to start asking as you cross A, or quick to the aids, in which case you may want to wait until you are definitely past A. Remember in the canter depart to keep your head up and your shoulders back, to sit into the canter, and to let your belly button lead. As you canter through your corner, look down the rail toward E. Just before E, half-halt your horse and allow him to feel your outside (left) corridor wall.

As you half-halt and ready your horse for the turn onto the circle, begin drawing your back-and-forth arc lines. First find your point on the centerline and draw a line in the sand back to you at E, then look at B and draw your line back to the centerline, then to the centerline of the second half of the circle back to B, and finally from E again back to the centerline. Draw this line back and forth a number of times to reinforce your path. As you complete your circle and approach E again, half-halt your horse and allow him to feel your inside (right) corridor wall as you look down the rail and prepare for your corner. As you approach H, draw your line from C back through the corner. Decide how deeply you will ride into the corner based on your horse's balance and your ability to support him. As you ride through this corner, look over to C and mentally prepare for your down transition to trot.

As you are riding through the corner, mentally prepare for your down transition by going over your down transition aids. How does your horse feel at this time? Will he need lighter or stronger aids to come down? Add this information about your horse to your preparation. Just before C, half-halt your horse both to regulate the canter and to give your horse a heads-up, then follow through with a down transition. As you make the transition to trot, open and strengthen your front, prepare to regulate the tempo if necessary, and look up toward M. Now draw your line from M back through the corner toward you. Decide on your path through the corner based on your horse's balance and your ability to support him. As you enter the corner, look down the rail toward B and begin mentally preparing for the walk transition.

As you approach B, keep your eyes up and play back each quarter or half circle in your mind as you ride the stretchy circle. Make sure to give the horse enough rein to allow him to put his nose below his knee, and to keep his throatlatch open. If you do not give him enough rein, he will simply curl. Regulate his trot tempo with your posting and his circle with your corridor walls. As you approach B again and begin to take up the reins, allow your horse to feel your inside (right) corridor wall and mentally prepare yourself to guide the horse down the rail toward F. While riding down the rail, look forward to the centerline in front of A and draw a line back toward A, over through the corner, and along the rail to you. While creating your path, keep in mind what tempo you will need to successfully navigate these two turns back to back, while still being able to support your horse and keep him in balance.

As you strengthen your outside corridor wall and keep your force field at the ready while looking down the centerline at the judge, prepare to soften your outside wall (left) and strengthen your inside (right) corridor so that the horse travels straight down the centerline. Have both force fields at the ready to keep him straight toward X as you use your video playback to draw your line. Before X, half-halt and then ask for a down transition, releasing so that he comes forward into the walk. Half-halt again, and then ask for a halt. Salute. Speak to the judge only when spoken to; otherwise, leave the arena at a walk on a long rein by continuing up to C, turning along the rail, and exiting at A.

Test Movements	Test 1, 6/15	Test 3, 7/1	Test 1, 7/22
Halt, entrance	5	7	8
Walk, medium	5	7	7
Walk, free	6	6	7
Walk/trot trans left	6	6	8
Walk/trot trans right	5	6	7
Trot, twenty meter circle left	6	6	7
Trot, twenty meter circle right	5	6	7
Trot, stretchy circle	5	5	8
Trot, diagonal	6	6	7
Trot loop left	6	6	6
Trot loop right	6	6	6
Canter depart left	5	5	5
Canter depart right	6	6	6
Canter, twenty meter circle left	5	6	6
Canter, twenty meter circle right	6	6	6
Canter, change rein through trot across diagonal	5	5	5
Canter/trot transition left	6	6	6
Canter/trot transition right	6	6	6
Halt, final	5	7	10

Appendix
Charting Your Scores

Competition should be not merely a way to collect ribbons and scores, but a valuable source of information about how you and your horse are progressing. In a general way, the collectives and the judge's final remarks can help you understand strengths and underlying problems, but it is also useful to analyze your scores for individual movements, so that you know, for example, whether your free walk is improving, or that you need more strength in the canter to the right. To help you group your movement scores across tests and through time, I have provided a printable table at manorminor.com. The first column lists all the movements found in the three training level tests, grouped according to gait. In the remaining columns, fill in the show, test, and date at the top, and then plug in your scores for each movement. After a number of shows, you should easily be able to see your strong and weak areas, and use this information to focus your training sessions.

Bibliography
Where Do We Read from Here?

There are many excellent books on dressage, but most of them cover the whole gamut from training level to grand prix. Even those that market themselves as introductory texts devote quite a bit of space to movements such as shoulder-in that do not appear until second level. There's no reason that you should not read these books; I think you should read as much as you can about this art, and knowledge of the larger arc of dressage training can help immensely while training at the lower levels. But our purpose here is to focus on what is most helpful to the training level rider.

Dr. Hilary Clayton has written a number of excellent books on the horse's biomechanics, but they are pricey. They are also quite technical. A more accessible option is the trilogy by Dr. Deb Bennet, *Principles of Conformation Analysis*. Susanne von Dietze's *Balance in Movement* is a comprehensive but somewhat dry disquisition on the rider's posture and balance and the functional anatomy of horse and rider. Sally Swift's books cover some of the same ground in a more readable way, with many helpful illustrations. Since the rider's core strength and balance are so vital, any good book on Pilates or the Alexander technique will be helpful.

There are many good books on gymnastic exercises, such as Jec Aristotle Ballou's *101 Dressage Exercises for Horse and Rider*, but in most relatively few exercises are meant specifically for the training level horse and rider pair. The excellent *Teaching Exercises*, by Major Anders Lindgren, is a notable exception.

We have a wealth of information from the great masters of the past. Alois Podhajsky's account of his experiences with various horses and famous people, *My Horses, My Teachers*, underscores the discipline, humility, and love of horses found in all the great masters. Though Gustav Steinbrecht's *Gymnasium of the Horse* is typical in that it covers a wide swath of dressage training, its depth of knowledge has earned its status as my favorite horse book of all time.

Xenophon wrote adequately on a great number of subjects, much as a journalist might do today, but he was not specifically a master of equitation. While it is commonplace to mention him, his writings serve more as evidence of the historical depth of serious thought on horse training than as practical training advice for the contemporary rider. Still, reading him still gives us a kick, to feel ourselves part of a tradition that is at least a few thousand years old.

For a contemporary approach I would mention Mary Wanless. Her books can be chewy and slow going to read, but they are worth the effort. And though she is often described as a little outside of the mainstream, I think her vantage as someone who is not a great natural rider but has struggled is invaluable for all of us everyday people. *Ride with Your Mind Essentials* is the most accessible starting point for anyone interested in her books.

Other contemporary writers worth exploring include Paul Belasik, a classicist who emphasizes the philosophical aspect of dressage; Lendon Gray, who offers commonsense practical information for training level in her *Lessons with Lendon*; Carl Hester, one of the best of the modern competitive school; and Betsy Steiner, a devotee of Pilates for the rider.

Finally, I would like to make a few comments on dressage schools in general. Obviously, those of us engaged in dressage theory can spend years discussing the nuances, but in very general terms there are two main camps. The classical school is often associated with France and the Cadre Noir, Iberia, and Austria and the Spanish Riding School. It emphasizes balance and self-carriage first, before concentrating on forward movement, an approach that often results in lighter rein contact. Proponents of this school have a deep appreciation for the history of dressage and for the haute école movements not found in modern competition. Baroque horses such as the Andalusian or Lipizzan are well suited to the classical training system.

The modern school is often associated with Germany, and reflects that nation's influence on contemporary competitive dressage. This school emphasizes forward movement into the bridle, often resulting in a relatively firmer contact initiated by the horse, and seeks to develop balance through the rider's aids and by building the horse's strength. The modern school emphasizes the quality of elasticity in the horse's movements, and cultivates the extended as well as the collected gaits. Warmblood breeds such as the Hanoverian and Dutch Warmblood fit well into a modern training program.

Many riders take a little from both schools, and of course warmbloods can be trained in the classical method, just as baroque horses can be trained in the modern method. At this point in your dressage training, I would suggest that you keep an open mind, and appreciate what both schools add to our understanding of the horse.

Made in the USA
Lexington, KY
24 February 2015